shaping the fractured self

fractured

self

POETRY OF CHRONIC ILLNESS AND PAIN

First published in 2017 by
UWA Publishing
Crawley, Western Australia 6009
www.uwap.uwa.edu.au
UWAP is an imprint of UWA Publishing
a division of The University of Western Australia

National Library of Australia Cataloguing-in-Publication entry

Title: Shaping the fractured self : poetry of chronic illness and pain / edited by Heather Taylor Johnson.
ISBN: 9781742589312 (paperback)
Notes: Includes bibliographical references.
Subjects: Healing--Poetry.
Poetry--Psychological aspects.
Australian poetry--21st century.
Other Creators/Contributors: Johnson, Heather Taylor, editor.

Printed by Lightning Source
Cover design and typeset by Carolyn Brown www.tendeersigh.com.au
Cover image by Elena Ray www.shutterstock.com

This project has been assisted by the South Australian government through Arts South Australia.

shaping the fractured self

POETRY OF CHRONIC ILLNESS AND PAIN

EDITED BY
HEATHER TAYLOR JOHNSON

To Dwight Johnson

CONTENTS

FOREWORD

'Sometimes pus, sometimes a poem…but always pain', the Israeli poet Yehuda Amichai wrote, a near-perfect poetic distillation of the costs of creativity, at least 'sometimes'.

Of course not all great art has its genesis in pain, and not all pain – not even a fraction – leads to the partial consolations of art. But if lancing an abscess is the surest way to healing, can poetry offer that same cleansing of emotional wounds?

At least – again – 'sometimes'.

The Ancient Greeks thought so. *Katharsis* – 'cleansing' – is a concept central to Aristotle's view of tragedy. Aeschylus, eldest of the three great Athenian tragedians whose work has survived, put it best. His masterpiece *Agamemnon*, first of the 'boxed-set' of dramas that make up the Oresteian trilogy, offers another near-perfect poetic distillation: this time of the costs of wisdom, of 'learning through suffering'.

Aeschylus knew a bit about physical and emotional suffering: he fought against the Persians in the Battle of Marathon; his brother was killed in that battle. Like all writing that matters, at least emotionally, his plays were hard-won.

Were they also therapeutic – either for him or his audiences?

In the modern era (if we can regard Josef Breuer and Sigmund Freud as modern) 'catharsis' has become a psychoanalytic term, which again emphasises the connection between art and healing.

There are plenty of cathartic moments, and much hard-earned wisdom and hard-wrung poetry in the pages that follow – and also much beautiful and consolatory writing. Since the writers can speak for themselves more eloquently – and more expansively – than I can on their behalf, I might finish with a quote from a writer who isn't represented, Inga Clendinnen, but who happened to die today, while I was writing this piece and thinking about suffering.

Clendinnen's book, *Tiger's Eye*, is one of the great memoirs of illness; its words surely speak to, and for, most of the fine writers Heather Taylor Johnson has gathered here.

Illness granted me a set of experiences otherwise unobtainable. It liberated me from the routines which would have delivered me, unchallenged and unchanged, to discreet death. Illness casts you out, but it also cuts you free. I will never take conventional expectations seriously again, and the clear prospect of death only makes living more engaging.[1]

Peter Goldsworthy

1   I. Clendinnen, *Tiger's Eye: a Memoir*, Melbourne: Text Publishing, 2010, p. 288.

NOTE FROM THE EDITOR

When I first tried to write poetry about my illness, it was clumsy and maddening. I questioned why that might be and began researching my addiction and adversity to it. What I gathered is that I wasn't alone; it's difficult to transcribe bodily trauma and maybe that's why there's not much literature – poetry, especially – about chronic illness or pain to be found. I did, however, discover an enormous and outstanding anthology from the United States called *Articulations: the Body and Illness in Poetry* edited by Jon Mukand. Totalling more than 400 pages, it's like a Bible for people living with illness, particularly those who love poetry – people exactly like me. It frightened me that a book so important might one day fall out of circulation, and I wondered if I could do something similar to it in Australia and add to the canon of illness narrative in poetry. I wondered if I could gather together twenty or so poets (it turned out to be twenty-eight) who might offer solace to one another and to their nameless readers who, like me, might read poetry in the bath after the body's been through a particularly draining day, or before turning off their light at night, wanting comfort to be their last feeling before facing total darkness.

I imagined big things and told my friend Andy Jackson about all of them: poetry, chosen anonymously, but three poems by each poet because as our conditions shift from day to day, as our *emotions* shift from day to day, so should the way we present them; and a contextualising statement, so that the poetry itself needn't be bogged down by explanation – besides, a contextualising statement would be another way to narrate an illness, which was exciting and opened up possibilities. Did I want to include carers and medical practitioners? Definitely. These people need a voice, too, and chronicity needs their perspective. Did I want to include cancer patients? There seemed to be a lot of this poetry out there already, almost a genre in and of itself, and as the submissions began trickling in, I quickly realised cancer has every right to be represented in this anthology and I'm sorry there isn't more of this poetry, as with AIDS and so many other diseases and conditions that go unmentioned. Did I want to include disability? This seemed to be a unique topic and one I wasn't sure I had the right to foster. Andy asked me if I'd read *Beauty is a Verb: the New Poetry of Disability*, which I hadn't, and I ordered it immediately and loved it. Sheila Black, Jennifer Bartlett and Michael Northen, as editors, had the same concept I was developing in terms of a work of prose contextualising the accompanying poems, and they pulled it off beautifully (the cover is absolutely stunning, I might add).

I am thrilled – *unequivocally* thrilled – that *Shaping the Fractured Self: Poetry of Chronic Illness and Pain* sits beside *Beauty is a Verb* as well as Mukand's *Articulations*. I hope it's one of many poetry books in a long line to come out of illness and pain, disability and mental health, cancer, postnatal depression, and ageing and dementia narratives because rhythm, spacing, enjambment and choice of or lack of punctuation, every metaphor and indentation and every move toward experimentation carries great weight when representing the fracturing of the body and the de(con)struction of the self. I applaud poetry as pathography and I congratulate every poet who is brave enough to go there. Please, enjoy.

Heather Taylor Johnson

'UNDISCOVERED COUNTRIES':
AN INTRODUCTION TO
SHAPING THE FRACTURED SELF

RACHEL ROBERTSON

What does it mean to be ill?

This seemingly simple question is, in fact, a complex conundrum, both for the individual and society. It is a question not answerable solely through medical language. Medicine rarely helps us understand pain and suffering, or learn to live with uncertainty and fragility. We may understand *illness* through a medical lens but the *illness experience* must be understood using other tools including, and especially, literature.

In 1926, Virginia Woolf lamented the lack of literature about illness.

> Considering how common illness is, how tremendous the spiritual change that it brings, how astonishing, when the lights of health go down, the undiscovered countries that are then disclosed, what wastes and deserts of the soul a slight attack of influenza brings to light, what precipices and lawns sprinkled with bright flowers a little rise of temperature reveals, what ancient and obdurate oaks are uprooted in us in the act of sickness...when we think of this and infinitely more, as we are so frequently forced to think of it, it becomes strange indeed that illness has not taken its place with love, battle, and jealousy among the prime themes of literature. Novels, one would have thought, would have been devoted to influenza; epic poems to typhoid; odes to pneumonia, lyrics to toothache.[2]

Although Woolf ignored the presence of illness in the works of writers such as the Brontës as well as the Romantics' linkage of madness with creativity,

....

2   V. Woolf, 'On Being Ill', *New Criterion*, January 1926, p. 32.

she was right to identify a strange lack of writing about illness, particularly given she was producing this essay less than a decade after the flu pandemic of 1918.

It was not until the middle of the twentieth century that illness narratives began to be published in larger numbers and accounts of Woolf's 'undiscovered countries' began to reach the reading public. According to Anne Hunsaker Hawkins, the 1950s saw the emergence of biographical pieces about the 'last illnesses' of famous people and autobiographical works by illness survivors, particularly those with polio.[3] The biggest growth of autobiographical writing about illness, however, occurred in the 1980s and 1990s, with works about HIV/AIDS and breast cancer kickstarting the trend towards non-famous individuals publishing their own illness stories. Since then, there have been numerous narratives published in the English language, covering many different illnesses, chronic conditions and disabilities. This century, the growth of social media has also enabled people to self-publish using blogs, Facebook and other social media. These works, I would argue, are primarily ways for individuals to try to understand and communicate their own illness experiences. And these illness narratives have readers and, now, academics examining and theorising the field.

Writing is pattern-making. We find words and sentences and paragraphs to order our experiences, make sense of them, and assemble some sort of meaning for ourselves (and others). The onset of an illness, disability or chronic condition creates the need for a new pattern because the individual's previous life is shattered.[4] As Lisa Diedrich suggests, 'Illness enacts a transformation, a crisis of the subject, a crisis of subjectification itself'.[5] The individual no longer feels the same; she is not at home in her own life any longer. Kristen Lang in this book describes being diagnosed with anorexia at thirteen as 'a loss-of-identity moment that would haunt me for the next decade. And beyond.'[6] Her poem demonstrates this in phrases such as:

....

3   A. H. Hawkins, *Reconstructing Illness: Studies in Pathography*, West Lafayette: Purdue University Press, 1999.

4   I include illness and disability here not to conflate the two or suggest that disability is the same as illness at all. But, while distinct in concept, disability and illness may coexist in an individual and very often do.

5   L. Diedrich, 'Treatments: Negotiating Bodies, Language and Death in Illness Narratives', PhD Thesis, 2001, p. 16.

6   Kristen Lang, 'My Own Other Self', p. 147.

'In the small house of her body, / under the flooring, the crossbeams / have buckled.'[7]

If we recognise that our body is our home and deeply interwoven with our sense of self or identity, we can begin to understand the profound nature of the change to our sense of self that occurs when the body undergoes a major shift. Illness is very often an experience of fracture or disordering. Language can help to reassemble and reorder our experience. The telling, even more the writing, of an illness experience allows the individual the opportunity to reassert some agency and control over his own life.

When illness disrupts, we may imagine healthcare as a repairing mechanism. This is not always the case: in many instances, medical treatments are as difficult to endure as the illness itself and the controlling technologies of medicine can seem to steal the individual's autonomy as much as the illness. Once again, we see an oscillation between order and chaos, coherence and incoherence. Medical treatment may also be experienced as lonely and depersonalised: what Andy Jackson describes as 'that strange distancing intimacy of medical treatment'.[8] This is not to suggest that healthcare workers create that distance (though this sometimes happens), but rather the process of treatment is often one of estrangement from one's self and others, in a hospital or alone at home, sometimes without others to share the experience. To re-personalise the depersonalising illness experience may be another reason to write about an illness.

The drive to write about illness, then, appears to come from a changed sense of self and the desire to create a form of personal order out of complex and confusing experiences. But this order can never be the old version of life; serious or chronic illness rarely allows for what Thomas Couser calls a 'rhetoric of triumph' or what Arthur Frank describes as a 'restitution narrative'.[9] One of the challenges of writing about illness is the difficulty of narrating indeterminacy, of connecting past, present and future when the past no longer seems relevant and the present has highlighted the

....

7 Kristen Lang, 'The small house of her body', p. 151.

8 Andy Jackson, 'World in a Grain of Flesh', p. 33

9 G. Thomas Couser, 'Conflicting Paradigms: the Rhetorics of Disability Memoir', in J. C. Wilson and C. Lewiecki-Wilson (eds), *Embodied Rhetorics: Disability in Language and Culture*, Carbondale and Edwardsville: Southern Illinois University Press, 2001, pp. 78–91; A. Frank, *The Wounded Storyteller: Body, Illness and Ethics*, Chicago: University of Chicago Press, 1995.

..gency and unknowability of the future. As David Carr says, 'The present is only possible for us if it is framed and set off against a retained past and a potentially envisaged future'.[10]

A further challenge of writing about illness is that the experience of illness and pain seems alien to words. Woolf talks about 'the poverty of the language' and Elaine Scarry asserts that 'physical pain does not simply resist language but actively destroys it'.[11] Although Scarry is primarily talking about acute pain (as experienced in torture, for example), it is often contended that pain is impossible to convey in language. For those without a clear medical diagnosis, finding language is challenging for other reasons. Not having words or a framework for what is happening to you is deeply troubling. In this anthology, Fiona Wright notes, '[M]y body was betraying me, and I dragged it around from clinic to consulting room', while struggling to find a diagnosis.[12]

The difficulty of expressing pain and the discontinuity of illness mitigate against representation – in prose at any rate. In 2002, Shlomith Rimmon-Kenan found very few published 'fragmented' illness narratives and asked, 'Wouldn't narrative fragmentation be the most suitable form for the experience of disrupted narrative identity?'[13] It is perhaps no surprise, then, that recent writing about illness has involved forms such as the lyric essay, various hybrid forms and poetry, as in this volume. Where prose narratives work with time, continuity, and cause and effect, poetry and lyric forms can work with fragments and space, and processes of reiteration and accretion. Poetry, with its use of metaphor and metonymy, creates meaning through suggestion and evocation. It tolerates, even creates, uncertainty and ambiguity. Poetry, then, may be the perfect form to reflect the complexity of the individual illness experience. In his book *Poetry as Survival*, Gregory Orr writes:

> Human culture 'invented' or evolved the personal lyric as a means
> of helping individuals survive the existential crises represented by

10 D. Carr, *Time, Narrative and History*, Bloomington: Indiana University Press, 1991, p. 60.
11 V. Woolf, 'On Being Ill', p. 34; E. Scarry, *The Body in Pain: the Making and Unmaking of the World*, Oxford: Oxford University Press, 1985, p. 4.
12 Fiona Wright, 'From Clinic to Consulting Room', p.104
13 S. Rimmon-Kenan, 'The Story of "I": Illness and Narrative Identity', *Narrative*, 10.1, 2002: 9–27, p. 19.

extremities of subjectivity and also by such outer circumstances as poverty, suffering, pain, illness, violence, or loss of a loved one. This survival begins when we 'translate' our crisis into language – where we give it symbolic expression as an unfolding drama of self and the forces that assail it.[14]

Taking this idea further, Stephen Kuusisto argues that the 'lyric poem or essay is brief…and both nearly always arise from a crisis in the writer's life'.[15] He suggests that the 'lyric mode is concerned with momentum rather than certainty', arguing that 'the gnomon of lyric consciousness' is that 'darkness can be navigated'.[16] The idea of momentum here is important, as it allows for the agency of the writer, and suggests how the writer reworks the crisis of subjectivity that illness calls forth. As Rachael Guy puts it: 'Through poetry I am finding the *particular* language for my "atypical" body….I give voice to the discord, ambivalence, inconvenience, fear and beauty of this corporeal existence.'[17]

The short personal statements (some of them like lyric essays) and the poems in this volume attest to the ability of the lyric mode to traverse darkness and give it symbolic expression. Here, personal illness experiences are transmuted into forms that reflect the damaged, suffering and resilient body. What Frank calls the 'chaos narrative' – 'an anti-narrative of time without sequence, telling without mediation, and speaking about oneself without being fully able to reflect on oneself'[18] – is not disavowed here but rather given a voice through the lyric mode in a way that both represents and transcends chaos. In the oscillation between order and disorder, the poets here represent both devastation and survival, and display 'both rupture and beauty' to our view.[19]

And what are we, as readers, to do with such a view? How do we navigate the darkness and light we read in this collection of deeply personal and

14 G. Orr, *Poetry as Survival*, Athens, GA: The University of Georgia Press, 2002, p. 4.
15 S. Kuusisto, 'Walt Whitman's "Specimen Days" and the Discovery of the Disability Memoir', *Prose Studies: History, Theory, Criticism*, 27:1–2, 2005: 155–62, p. 155.
16 S. Kuusisto, 'Walt Whitman's "Specimen Days"', p. 161.
17 Rachael Guy, 'The Condition'' p.188.
18 A. Frank, *The Wounded Storyteller*, p. 98.
19 A. Jurecic, *Illness as Narrative*, Pittsburgh, PA: University of Pittsburgh Press, 2012, p. 109.

yet universal works? What response is called forth from us when we read this collection of 'things more / beautiful for having been broken', as Anne M Carson's poem puts it?[20]

First, I think, we are asked to experience pleasure when reading this book. Like Woolf's 'precipices and lawns sprinkled with bright flowers', there is much to enjoy in these poems. They sing on the page, inviting us into a place of sharp observation, potent language and delicate sensibility. Who wouldn't feel joy at reading lines such as 'You said melancholy, I said Chopin', or 'He offers to feed you / spoonfuls of himself', or 'descent into / the dark thighs of your cave'?[21] This book can be relished in the way all good poetry is enjoyed.

We can also experience the particular pleasure of reading the authors' introductory statements alongside their poetry. These statements provide a context for the poetry but also act as a kind of personalising mechanism. Their overtly autobiographical tone and direct disclosure of personal experiences bind the reader to the writers, creating, I suggest, an unwritten contract or agreement between reader and writer. The authors' disclosures focus our attention, encourage us to read with care and thoughtfulness. Reading, especially reading poetry, slows us down. We have time to contemplate what we read, to experience vicariously what the writer has shown us. On reading this volume, illness no longer 'falls outside the thinkable' (as Michel de Certeau says of the dying).[22] This is surely good because it encourages empathy and prepares us for our own and our loved ones' future experiences of illness.

In her work on narrative medicine, Rita Charon describes how attention and representation lead to a sense of affiliation.[23] By reading, with attention, the representation of illness in these poems and author statements, we can recognise our affiliation with each other, our shared lives as human beings, and, perhaps, our shared responsibilities. We may find ourselves developing a more empathetic and creative response to our own and other people's illnesses.

....

20 Anne M Carson, 'Axiology', p. 20.

21 Anne M Carson, ': meditations on melancholy' p. 21; Heather Taylor Johnson, 'The Sick Room', p. 102; Susan Hawthorne, 'descent', p. 73.

22 Michel de Certeau says, 'the dying man *falls* outside the *thinkable*' (emphasis in original) in *The Practice of Everyday Life* (S. Rendall, Trans.), Berkeley: University of California Press, 1984, p. 90.

23 See for example, R. Charon, 'Narrative Medicine: Attention, Representation, Affiliation', *Narrative*, 13.1, 2005, pp. 261–70.

Illness and caring for the ill are often viewed as intimate matters that occur in the private or domestic sphere or within a liminal institution such as a hospital. We recognise healthcare planning as a matter of public policy but in practice tend to leave individuals to manage their own health within a family setting. As Sid Larwill notes in his author statement, 'Illness pushed us out of the mainstream'.[24] Perhaps these poems question our assumptions about the proper relationship of the public and private? We are invited into private spaces of suffering and of hope and asked to take that knowledge out into the world.

The paradox at the heart of an illness experience is that it is both highly intimate and profoundly estranging. *Shaping the Fractured Self* shows us how to create meaning in the face of life's loneliness, uncertainty and fragility. It demonstrates that the sick body is also, as Quinn Eades here claims, 'the strong body, the fighting body, the body brave enough to dis-organise, to be in excess. The sick body is the body that knows it is dying, and turns towards that moment, and insists on being seen'.[25] The writers here have particular knowledge and are sharing this with us. As Arthur Frank says, 'illness is privileged in the fullness of its participation in life—although, most people have to be sick to realize that'.[26] The reader of this book doesn't need to be ill to enjoy this fullness; we can experience it vicariously, poetically. This book commands our attention and offers us a gift – works of art that express a deep engagement with life, and all of Woolf's 'undiscovered countries' therein.

....

24 Sid Larwill, 'Creeping up on the Things that Matter', p. 162.
25 Quinn Eades, 'Fragment: the Body Writing in Excess''' p. 139.
26 A. Frank, 'Five Dramas of Illness', *Perspectives in Biology and Medicine*, 50:3, summer 2007, p. 380.

'EVEN AFTER BREAKING'

ANNE M CARSON

'Art does not see us but we see it, and can know that it has seen,
if not us, our condition. The likes of us. Maybe enough.'
– *Marion Halligan,* The Fog Garden

Poems are packed full of consciousness. Flannery O'Connor said she doesn't
know what she thinks until she has read what she has written. We are never
quite in control of the creative process – if it is any good there is always
something mysterious in its making. But for me, poems often grow out of
an engagement with specific ideas or images. Chronic illness and dis-ease
have provided such stimulus, having been interwoven with much of my
adult life, mostly through being a carer for others, but also through my own
encounters with chronic dis-ease. Chronic illness, however we meet it, is
profoundly challenging, and my encounters have forced me into a deep, life-
giving inquiry, partly undertaken through writing poems.

I have a sensitive nervous system. On the one hand, this allows for the
kind of intimations which often turn into poetry; on the other, it has also
led to some prolonged episodes of anxiety – the last prompted by the events
leading to the death of my husband in 2012.

One generative idea has been pivotal in my experience of chronic pain
and illness, both in myself and in my role as carer. It is the Winnicottian
idea of being *held* and *holding*. Donald Winnicott, an English paediatrician
and psychoanalyst, uses it to refer first to the holding a mother does of her
foetus in utero; then holding in arms by the mother or mother substitute;
then in ever-widening circles of holding through intimacy and friendship
to adult self-holding of our own needs and self, particularly when we are in
distress or pain.

Mindfulness meditation has provided an active way of implementing this
idea of holding. It helps me deal with the powerlessness engendered both
by my chronic conditions (including daily pain from premature arthritis)

as well as when witnessing a loved one's suffering, both in accepting powerlessness and in using whatever power is available to me.

In meditation I learn to discern what attitude I hold towards whatever I am experiencing. Whilst perfectly normal to tighten in resistance to pain or discomfort – one's own or others' – I have found that tightening exacerbates difficulties. This style of meditation develops the capacity for acceptance: just sitting (or lying) with the experience, and the in-and-out breath, and finding if, in that moment, it can be consented to with compassion, softening and acceptance. It is often challenging and sometimes all I can do is accept that, for now, I am in resistance. But on many occasions, it is supremely liberating and I have found that both psychic and even physical pain have melted. Sometimes our attitude is the only thing over which we can exert any control.

But it is not always appropriate to consent and not resist. In caring for others it has been essential to learn how to continue to hold myself whilst I have been caring for the other. I have found that resentment is an excellent teacher. When I see suffering or distress, particularly in loved ones, it is very hard not to dive in to try to help. But sometimes help is not wanted, nor do I always have the wherewithal to offer effective assistance. Learning my limits has helped me hold inner boundaries, be more truly myself, not to overreach and, when I care, be more confident my caring comes from a place of genuine generosity.

Writing offers another receptacle for the holding of psychic energy. This is useful for the writer who can pour herself – her flawed, in-the-process-of-coming-to-grips-with self – into her work. But when synergy happens, and the magic of alchemy infuses one's work, writing becomes a piece of art, perhaps of use to a reader too.

When I discovered the Japanese ceramic technique *kintsukuroi* (which forms the basis of my poem '*Axiology*'), I immediately translated it into psychological terms, marvelling at what a superbly redemptive image it is. The gold restores to the vessel its capacity to hold once again, not in denial of it having been fractured but even made beautiful because of it. The image partners so well with the Leonard Cohen quote and together they hold (as the poem's title suggests) a concept of great and poignant beauty for me.

Axiology

If I was ceramic I'd be *kintsukuroi*,
pottery which has been knocked,
dropped, broken into shards then
mended with gold or silver lacquer,
a delicate meander of liquid gold
flowing into the breach. *Kintsukuroi* –
the word a whole world, evoking
the kind of place where mending
is valued more than the break,
where old is treasured more than
new, where putting things back
together is an art form, things more
beautiful for having been broken.

....

: meditations on melancholy

You said melancholy, I said Chopin; a poultice
you could put on pain. Dark notes held by beauty

in a soft hand. Not cry-your-eyes-out, slumped
in blurs of despond. But clear-eyed chords;

elegiac philosophy carried on rivers of soul.
Comfort for the bloody business of loss,

the carnage of having what is as close to you
as your own limb, lopped. The nocturnes lasso

darkness with light; ever-widening stories to which
your tale belongs. The simple peace when pain

is consented to. Silos of silence to sink in.

Splosh

You are out of your
element. When I pick

up your fish body
limbs dangle limp

in my arms. In water
just a twitch makes

you supple. Your bent
body floats free.

Exposed to air you
cramp, spasm, recoil

when touched.
Except by her – she

is your water – you
swam in her first.

'CHILDHOOD POLIO AND BEYOND: MY EXPERIENCE OF ILLNESS AND POETRY'

PETER BOYLE

It was 15 August 1954, the Feast of the Assumption, a little less than a month before my third birthday, when I woke up in an extreme fever, unable to walk. A doctor who was called to the house gave me an injection in my right buttock but the fever got worse. Soon polio was diagnosed and I was placed in solitary confinement in hospital.

The polio originally affected most of my body and I was still in an iron frame, able to move little more than my neck and arms, when I was released from hospital just before Christmas. My first real memory of life is perhaps ten months after this when we moved house. I remember the green station wagon, the leaves overhead, the Melbourne sun and later my father carrying me around the backyard of the new house. As in the poem I wrote many years later, 'Paralysis', it is a happy memory of great safety and wonder.

Within a few years muscle control returned to all of my body except my right leg, which remained withered and paralysed. I learned to walk, and continue to walk, using a caliper. Of course I was left out of sport and looked, and felt, different from other children my age. Then there was the impact of the time in hospital – not just the initial four or five months in an isolation ward at age three, but numerous operations to try to improve my stability and muscle control. The last of these was in Sydney when I was eleven, my first year of high school. I was in hospital for eight weeks and recuperating at home for a further eight weeks. I remember the nightmares and the terror of the dark from my time in hospital, but there was also an immense determination to learn, to explore the world, to achieve something special that would make up for my illness. I taught myself Latin while in hospital and, though a year younger than my classmates, excelled in my studies, especially languages, history and English, winding up dux of my high school, Riverview, in 1968. I also began writing poetry.

The self I had constructed to overcome my sense of disability was above all a bookish, academic self; however, over the course of my years at university,

23

this began to unravel. In 1972 I broke up with my girlfriend, dropped out of university and slid rapidly into depression. I returned the following year to complete English Honours, then did a Diploma of Education the year after and began teaching. High school teaching, overseas travel and depression alternated through my twenties and early thirties, but throughout it all was the dream of becoming a writer – a poet, a novelist or both. There were many factors in my depression but undoubtedly my sense of inferiority as a male, linked to my caliper and my long time of apartness, contributed to it. There was also the restlessness prompted by my desire to write, my failure to write and my fantasy of discovering the right place that would transform me. In part, my restlessness was the product of a sense that I had to achieve something really big to make up for my disability, that there must be a flipside, a remarkable destiny that would be the compensation for all of my own – and my parents' – suffering.

By my late thirties, with marriage, children and a fulfilling job as a TAFE teacher, I had largely got beyond the depression, and within a year of marriage, from 1988 onwards, the poems started to come. Many of them used images and phrases stored up in me over the previous thirty to forty years. Some of them, like 'Separation', 'Kinderszeit', 'For my father' and 'Paralysis', from my first three books, drew on my childhood experiences, especially my time in hospitals.

In 2006 I learned that I had prostate cancer and a serious, life-threatening form of it. The turmoil of those times and the grim encounter with my own mortality are present in some of the poems in *Apocrypha* (2009) and in the long poem 'In the sleep of the riverbed' from *Towns in the Great Desert* (2013). The last poem from the 'Towns in the Great Desert' sequence describes a dream I had after the prostatectomy, coming to terms with the damage to my virility – a vision of the immense beauty there is in life regardless of how much is taken away.

Late in 2014 we learned that my partner had multiple myeloma, a particularly virulent form of cancer affecting the blood and the bones. It was already at a fairly advanced stage, and the chemotherapy needed was drastic. Instead of growing old together as we had imagined, serious chronic illness became our reality. This is not my illness to write about but it is a hammerblow. For months a sense of numbness overwhelmed me. I'm a writer and a poet and writing is what keeps me strong. Yet, what to write? In these circumstances, how to write at all?

For the past three years I had been working on a project called

Ghostspeaking, a book of imaginary poets from Latin America and France, where I invented poets, gave them biographies and wrote their poems. I invented a character, Ernesto Ray, a poet from Puerto Rico, who starts life as a New York singer and rapper but gives it all away, first to be a Buddhist, then later to write a thin book of poems as magic spells of blessing for his wife Pauline who is dying of cancer. A very late uncollected poem of Ray's is 'Hammerblows'. While the other poems of Ray's were attempts to project blessings, this one, I think, lets out the emotions of grief, anger and bewilderment.

In *Ghostspeaking* there is also a collection of prose poems attributed to 'the Montaigne poet', an anonymous man or woman who has a rather philosophic bent and writes in a mix of prose poetry and essay. Through him or her I sometimes transform dreams I have had. 'On the eternal nature of fresh beginnings' is a poem I wrote rapidly in the middle of one night. It was a voice speaking out of me and I simply had to listen carefully as it spoke. It felt like part of the psyche breaking through the numbness, offering consolation but more than consolation, a clear seeing into the goodness and beauty at the core of life. One of poetry's great tasks is to give voice to that 'clear seeing'. Insofar as we can be in touch with that reality, then illness, suffering, disease, are not the whole of the story.

Paralysis

Laid out flat
in the back of the station wagon my father borrowed
I look up:
the leaves are immense,
green and golden with clear summer light
breaking through –
though I turn only my neck
I can see all of them
along this avenue that has no limits.

What does it matter
that I am only eyes
if I am to be carried
so lightly
under the trees of the world?
From beyond the numbness of my strange body
the wealth of the leaves
falls forever
into my small still watching.

....

Hammerblows

'Hay golpes en la vida, tan fuertes. . .Yo no sé!'
– *César Vallejo*

In subway cars
on a path below high mountains
storm coming down
in the 10 a.m. sun moving step by step
along a row of chairs lined up on a sidewalk
in the name on an envelope
under a thick smear of jam
in the suicide of buttons in a drawer of waiting knives
There are blows

In what you know hear want can't say
fecund snowflake razors
there are blows

In the breeze that rises
when someone's gone
In airports and the chill eternal
failure to set out
In the rewiring of memories
so every landscape every half-arsed jerking of
an ill-timed word
floods all the avenues
rains like ripe tomatoes
on the most umbilical umbrellas
there are blows

Like the sleek geek who won't speak
rancid skies dripping death
like petrified vultures oozing lard
in the forecourts of the Four Winds Stock Exchange
or a banker on hard times sniffing glue that oozes
from a pothole of pock-marked
preferences to trade in the dark

Unarguably
there are blows
A tree to the knees
A quick slit to the left of the breath
A brief stab to the right trapezoid
and it flows
like rum of the Rialto
gone sodden gone
drenched fire
hung from heaven on a wire
like a dream going forward
or a tack stuck in a throat
that won't pass
there are blows

Under benches
in safe cubicles
in a scrambled letter left behind on a train
in paper cups soiled plates
a fridge crammed with wedges of stale bread
or a road that twists its cracked spine under rain
there are blows
and in the imperceptible
accumulation of seconds
as a roof snaps
as a day drifts into darkness

in the flip of a card
in solitaire
in conversations morsed by the time-bleep of machines
in the crisp voice flooding like treacle
over the floor of an office
or the practised spiel rehearsing
the trajectory of endings
in our endings

Set upon by minions gagged by gargoyles
on the roof, feet kicking

drained of air like a deflated owl
crowd-surfed down corridors
dressed by ghost-fingers in
some tight-fitting cloak of lost arms
in the steady breath of midnight stillness
or the scratch-scratchings of pain rocking
on a makeshift trestle by the window under stars
my love
in every moan replayed
there are blows

In the trickle of the chicken that's rotting
in the shoulder-bag of the boy of the third strap
of the last carriage that wavers above the
          all blasted
             their hands nailed to iron rafters
and yet the light is there

In the land of far away last night
where an old tart flicks her foxtail bathrobe in your face
in the pissoirs of seventh heaven
where red pustules sprout from boys' flies
and a certain stench
clenches your nails on the zipper that won't budge
when you feel like a foetus growing old in a waterhole for ratsack
as the gaunt attorney
slips your fingerprints into the
state-owned deposition on the inventory
of purloined combs
that nails you there, right there
among tender ostriches
hanging by a thread

And there are blows
immaculate interceptions
disconnected calls to Mars
music that turns one last time at the threshold
turns back to gaze at us

once-only short-term spinners
left behind in the room for lost jars

like a wave going out
along the edge of the world
like some bleary-eyed bard of the doorway
who wears our face
and has no language

all the hammerblows it takes
to make a hammerklavier
the nails nailed into it
and when it soars
the still attentive fingers numbering death

and how
on the lowest edges of the heavenly choir
among the counsellors consolers
where the jackboots just now begin to reach
there are blows

How say it
beloved
now my face is
three swift kicks of death
on the night-patrol of nowhere
two hands round a thick jug gathering light
and yet and yet. . .

There are blows

On the eternal nature of fresh beginnings

This body next to you, said the German expert on design, is your ideal self – what you climbed out of once and have since forgotten about. Like gills and dialogues with rainbows, like your life as a ruminant quadruped, it has been erased from your waking story. When the time is right you will step inside it and it will transport you. Do not look at the claws that dangle from its withered right arm – consider only its wings. Say to yourself the word 'Perfection'. Be confident. All the stars of the universe were placed millennia ago far inside you.

'WORLD IN A GRAIN OF FLESH'

ANDY JACKSON

I came to poetry for two reasons – to try to feel at home outside the church, and to try to feel at home inside my own body. I was an awkward and sensitive teenager with an acute sense of injustice, a vague intuition of the interconnectedness of things and a desire to belong. A few of my friends were evangelical Christians. I found myself wanting to be born again, and joined them. But as the years went on, Christianity felt less and less convincing – its skin was sloughing off, the lenses of faith gathering dust. With tender skin and squinting eyes, I started writing what I later realised were poems. I was trying to contradict the certainties and turn the beliefs inside out, to see the life in the world as it is and embrace it.

Feeling at home outside the church turned out, for me, to be relatively easy. The body, however, is another thing entirely. This – our most intimate and only true possession, this enduring companion for our conscious life – can feel like something to be despised and disavowed.

I inherited Marfan syndrome from my father. Because of it, he died when I was two. For us, the body doesn't produce and process the protein fibrillin in the usual way. Like him, I am tall and thin, with long limbs and severe spinal curvature. Unlike him, at least so far, the valves of my heart haven't enlarged or weakened, which would put me at risk of aortic dissection. While the specific manifestations of Marfan vary greatly, all of us with the condition carry a heightened awareness of mortality and the stigma of physical difference.

My spine began to curve when I entered puberty. Surgery stabilised, but couldn't correct, it. I've had over thirty years now of inappropriate questions and assumptions, intrusive staring and casual abuse. At times, I consider it a badge of honour to be rejected by the small-minded. Other times, in fatigue and resentment, I've had enough, and I want out.

Almost fifteen years ago I found myself in the men's toilet of a Brunswick pub, shaking, almost weeping with relief and with the weight of years of otherness. I'd just read out the words of a new poem at the open mic – 'I have a hunch / that curvature / can be aperture / given that light, like water / does not travel in a straight line…' – and something in me had, painfully and beautifully, broken open. I had not only reclaimed a word that had been used against me, but I had suggested that 'deformity', rather than being a curse or a problem, is in fact the pre-eminent source of insight. Slowly, but surely, shame had begun to erode.

For me, poetry is one strand of the journey back into my own body, and therefore also into other lives. The three poems in this anthology are examples of that. The poem 'Nothing personal' looks back to my experience of surgery as a teenager, and that strange distancing intimacy of medical treatment. 'Whatever exists in the universe' is part of a suite of poems on medical tourism in India, and is an attempt to be faithful to India's ability to upset, enrage, hearten and confuse. 'Jess' is from *Music Our Bodies Can't Hold*, a forthcoming collection of poems – each of which is a portrait of someone with Marfan syndrome. I am indebted to Jess Marshall and all the other contributors for their generosity, honesty and humour.

Poetry seems to me a mode of writing particularly suited to deformity, to bodily otherness. It's incredibly subjective in origin, and thrives on idiosyncrasy and ambiguity. Poetry is also inherently social. When language is placed in the hands of people who have been marginalised, and then spoken in a public space, small transformations can be triggered. In a kind of collective neural plasticity, the connectivities between us are reinforced. The distinctions between us become more productive. It's something like empathy, but at its best, it's more like solidarity, felt in the bones and the heart.

Whether autobiographical, biographical or speculative, my poems are all experiments in visceral affinity. I want to evoke very particular bodily experiences and becomings – in my own and other voices – in the hope that something unexpected might arise, beyond the personal, and from within it. Or, to paraphrase William Blake, to see a world in a grain of flesh.

Nothing personal

He leans back against his desk, and asks
if, while he has me under, it would be worth
taking care of that leg too, pointing to it.
He is not talking to me, but my mother.
I'd rather not make this a bigger deal than it is,
so I say *don't bother*, to her,
who relays this across to the doctor.

~

The ceiling floods my head with whiteness.
Into the corner of my left eye, the television spits.
They've attached weights to my neck and ankles,
suspended them over both ends of the bed.
I will be like this for a week. Until I leave
in a brace with a spine-length scar,
I have only one red button to press.

~

The door is locked, the taps turned on.
Propped on a plastic chair, I am made wet
and clean by a nurse, still too fragile
to do it myself. As she leans over me,
the curtain of her uniform opens an inch,
briefly exposing a hint of the sensitive flesh
of our different positions, how cold it can be.

....

Whatever exists in the universe

Between the footpath and the road,
the shoe salesman unpacks his boxes again.
His son dusts
the three hundred pairs with a cloth
attached to a stick.

They're debating the latest Human Development Report
on *RSTV*. Malnutrition, sanitation, infrastructure –
it's hard to hear.   Diwali celebrations –
a war against night, a dense fog, smell of cordite.

They come seeking spiritual wisdom
                    and squalor, and find it.

    Five die, or more.
    The patients who survive
    get a thousand rupees each for their blindness.
    Expired eye drops, infected lenses.

Light breaks on the head of the destitute

The train rattles over the suburb, one storey up.
Near the mall, roofs are made of thatch
and banners from the last election –
a satellite dish balanced on the one concrete wall.
                    Crows compete over a rat.
One beak unspools the pink innards.

Yes, we understand how she's been behaving,
but if you want her to be admitted,
you will also have to pay for an attendant,
someone from the family.

He has no legs. He is crossing the road,
using his calloused hands,

                    moving slowly
towards the gutter, backwards.
An autorickshaw honks its protest
          or warning (who can tell?).

Arsenic, rising in the water-table
where the nation's rice is grown.

                  In nine months,
in Lucknow, three doctors found dead.
Each had been in charge
of the city's health budget.

When poverty comes, the ten vital airs fly off.

In 1814, a British surgeon gives up translating
Ayurvedic texts – their poetical style,
a banquet of absurdity to satisfy
the most voracious guest.

                Now, only
certain foreigners manage to overcome
all the obstacles necessary to reach India.
Westerners' psychological problems
regularly surface during treatment.
Their laughter often sounds like crying.

In suburban Chennai, a husband and wife

take poison, give sleeping pills to their two children.
Only Janani, three, severely retarded,
survives.

Yes, I keep forgetting, India has more millionaires
than any country. Why must we
focus on the negatives?

At the entrance to the ambulance bay, another shrine.
On the waiting room wall, a crucifix.
From the internet cafe, above the traffic, the call to prayer.
A man, on a nearby rooftop, does push-ups.
Whatever exists in the universe, exists in the human body.

They implant a pacemaker in her brain
when her body resists the medication.
No longer does she spend ten hours a day
washing off imaginary germs.

20,000 unlicensed medicine factories. Inspectors bribed. Up to 25% of pills
are fake. 1 child dies from encephalitis every 2 hours in Uttar Pradesh in
a single hospital. 3 children per incubator in an epidemic ward. Last year
60,000 women died during pregnancy or childbirth. 60% of the world's
undernourished children live in India. Numbers   stick in the throat.

Strangers catch sight of her deformed,
    fragmentary ear and stare. Anjali's
medical team sculpt for her a prosthetic one,
    complete with earring hole.

India is an extraordinary destination,
ideally suited for recovery and unwinding

after a stressful surgical intervention. Our after-care
healing programs not only replenish lost energy,
but also elevate it for spirited future living.

Sometimes I'm afraid all my scars will tear open
    or worse, that they already have.
The potholes are filled with broken bricks
and palm leaves. I don't want
   to get used to this
itch beneath bandages. And who
has qualms about preferential treatment when it's life
     or death?

Two men walk together, hands softly touching.
On TV – *below the skin you see*
is the skin you want.

After his death, the government hospital swells
with a crowd of family and friends,
smashing bottles, turning over tables,
screaming, throwing
     their grief against concrete walls.

To the patient, the doctor is a god.

A businessman in the restaurant, the empty
left arm of his pale green shirt.
Four floors up, the private clinic –
security guards chat by the door.
Three schoolgirls in immaculate uniforms
walk through the traffic, linked hand to shoulder.
The last in the line is blind.
    She takes small steps.

....

Jess

'I would be giving in to a myth of sameness which I think can destroy us.'
– Audre Lorde

sometimes I wake into a quiet sadness
blood pooling in my mouth
bones on fire – this is the worst
and best thing that has ever happened to me

one morning I couldn't walk
the white coats
gave me a chair – I became an adult
while they tried to work it out
the closest was *marfanoid habitus*
'til a sudden knife in the chest
gave me enough points for the full diagnosis
hearing it, I felt sick

I have mitral valve prolapse, regurgitation
multiple pulmonary nodules
I get short of breath and produce
excessive mucous (clearly I'm very attractive)
my joints are hypermobile
and dislocate (they go out more than I do)
I'm the walking rubber-band

comments and names at school
don't cross your legs, you look disgusting
spider-woman, anorexic slut
other things I can't write

doctors accused my parents of abuse
threatened me with feeding tubes
ironic, it was only all this pointing at my bones
that gave me an eating disorder

since I joined Chronic Illness Peer Support

they can't shut me up
we go on camps, socials, talk about whatever we need to
I meet the most incredible people
and call them my friends
(my dog helps me enormously with my grief)

I'm so motivated people find me exhausting
started studying nursing
but they told me I was too unwell
cried so hard I broke a rib – now it's psych

I haemorrhaged every day for eighteen months
clots bigger than my hand
doubled over in pain until I passed out
I think about my future a lot
imagine a husband, two golden retrievers
a blue house by the beach, veggie patch
all the people I will help
life is extraordinary and so are you

now look at this photo and tell me
you still want sameness

'TO BE SEEN OR NOT TO BE SEEN: COMING OUT AS UNWELL'

JESSICA COHEN

When I was twenty-four I visited a friend who was living on the Upper West Side of Manhattan. One winter evening, the slate skyline punctuated with New York's particular mosaic of buildings, we rugged up – two freezing Australians unused to navigating slippery pavement and cutting air – and set off up Broadway to find a tiny second-hand bookstore we'd heard of. Among the treasures were a stack of vintage postcards – all written on, stamped and sent – that had somehow been collected from all over America and deposited here in New York. On an impulse I selected a few with messages that appealed to me: some from the 1950s which told of one man's travels abroad; some from the 1960s detailing concerts seen, galleries visited, food eaten; and some perfunctory ones, the kind sent to appease anxious parents. From that day on, I took every opportunity to collect vintage postcards wherever I found them, vowing to be a keeper of strangers' memories. It occurred to me that in between the words on those cards lay intangible experiences that only existed in the memories and bodies of those who had lived them. And yet, the process of capturing them – pen on cardboard – offered an opportunity to hold onto a version of those experiences, even in their filtered state.

This is the gift which the written word offers: the opportunity to capture the elusive; to share one's most subjective, personal experiences; to attempt to present something muddled and intimate with clarity, and often beauty. Poetry, in particular, provides the option to share fragments and vignettes of distilled experiences which can serve to reduce a sense of internal isolation, and to encourage community and openness.

At twenty, I first began to 'come out' as dating women, a process which, rather exhaustingly, has proven to be continuous, anxiety-ridden and irritatingly repetitive. Back then it never occurred to me that in writing about my illness, and making it available to the public, I would face a second series of 'comings out' eight years later. And this is part of the abstract terrain those of us with 'invisible conditions' navigate.

My condition is fibromyalgia, a pain disorder caused by abnormalities in how pain signals are processed in the central nervous system. It is characterised by widespread pain in muscles, joints, nerves, inflammation and heightened pain responses to touch/sensation. The presence of constant pain can lead to secondary conditions such as disordered sleep, chronic fatigue and depression, which in turn can leave sufferers with chronic stomach, skin and immunity issues. From my earliest memories, I experienced hypersensitivity to sensation, and when I was twelve years old, I began to display the first obvious signs of fibromyalgia and had one attack of psoriatic arthritis in my hands. In the years that followed, the chronic pain and distortion of sensory output was accompanied by chronic fatigue syndrome. Perhaps most pertinent to my story are two factors: the condition is constant, and it is also invisible.

Being invisible can be lonely, isolating and frustrating. When there are no obvious demarcations to hint to the world that you are not functioning in full health, one can exist in an 'in-between' state where concessions and help are required, but rarely offered; and adjusting one's expectations of themselves, as well as the expectations of others, is an exhausting and disappointing reality.

However, 'coming out' as 'other' can also be a challenge. It requires one to advocate for her own needs, when she may not have fully accepted the limitations of her condition. And the prospect of placing what is, for many, a highly personal and private struggle into the public domain is daunting, to say the least. The level of vulnerability and openness required, mixed with a fear of the opinions of others, can seem worse than invisibility.

These illnesses can also leave a large gap between what is seen by others and what is known by the sufferer. This gap is easily filled by self-doubt, shame and guilt. Are we enough as we are? Will others think less of us if they know we are ill? Can we be loved and desired while also being unwell? How much of our condition do we accept? How much do we try to fight? In acceptance, is there room for hope? In acceptance, is there room for recovery?

For years, my greatest objective had been to avoid addressing these fears, and to create the illusion that my life was 'normal', that I was functioning as highly across every spectrum of it as all my friends appeared to be, and that my capacity to 'do' and 'achieve' matched a template of someone who was able-bodied. Plagued by self-consciousness and internalised self-stigmatisation, I fought an internal battle with my condition until my body could no longer hold me; a duel between body and soul, mind and matter. To ruminate on my condition would mean giving it airtime, which felt to me like defeat. So therefore, to write about it, was out of the question.

So what has changed for me? In part, it was watching a brave friend making her condition visible to her friends and family, and observing the wave of support that followed her announcement. Her 'coming out' revealed a strength of character, and a fierceness which I felt privileged to witness. Even in her unwell state, she carried an aura of strength and wholeness that can only arise from authenticity.

I have also come to realise that much like standing on the edge of a cold swimming pool, poised to jump, my fear of the cold is ameliorated by the knowledge that my body will ultimately acclimatise. And once the metaphorical acclimatisation happens, things that were once uncomfortable can become accepted and integrated.

'Coming out' is stepping out from a safe but uncomfortable silence, where difference is hidden, but one is safe. It is stepping into homogeny and holding up a placard that reads 'other' and hoping to be offered support rather than scorn. But it also provides an opportunity for greater dialogue around chronic illness. It aids in the destigmatisation of disabled bodies; and it helps to reinvent new templates for 'achievement' and 'success' that do not rest upon one paradigm of capacity.

I invite you to explore a small part of my lived experience and personal history with fibromyalgia and chronic fatigue syndrome.

....

Foundations I

I was born before I was ready.
Within the warm darkness,
I heard her muffled voice
And time became the hindering distance,
Only overcome by an act of boldness.

When the Earth's poles were equal distance from the sun,
Day and night meeting in measure
While orange and red leaves scattered the lawns
Of yawning suburban streets,
I made my move to join her.

But two months out of nine is a precious time,
Where hearts are made stronger,
And lungs are sealed
So that the tiny particles of loss and pain
That float in the air
Cannot be so easily breathed in.

Unformed, unprotected,
I inhaled,
Drawing deep into my body
The dying babies, the tubes, the machines.
And so the foundations of my being were laid
Pain and sensitivity woven into its fibres.

And the beauty of life,
Those delights sensed from within my mother's body –
The crunch of autumn leaves,
Muted melodies of voices, and warm heaviness of bodies,
The growing crispness in the air muddled with the incense of chimney
smoke –
Is now filtered through a layer of something
Thicker than her womb
Something ever-present.

Foundations II

When my foundations were laid
Somebody somewhere was distracted.
A faulty circuit spread through the length of me
Wires mismatched, currents misfiring.

Fuses tripped all the time.
'Stop it! It hurts!'
Tears through laughter
As the tickles of my older brothers
Hit my ribs with the sharpness of claws.

Pain came in sparks
Currents hurling through my body
The scooping delight of my father's hugs,
His musky smell blanketing me in contentment
Until the touch of fingers to arms
Shocked me with pain,
As real and true as my love for him.

But still there were horse rides
Trees climbed
Years of skipping through
Tanbark-filled playgrounds.
Until Saturday morning aged twelve
Slippered feet pattering across the kitchen
Winnie the Pooh pyjamas and tangled hair
With hands supporting my neck,
The fibres began to burn out.

The waiting room

The chairs in this waiting room are hard.
Narrow and hard,
Like chairs in a high school
Designed to keep students from falling asleep.

My ankles rest on one another.
I shift.
They part, widen again.
Fingers placed in the ridges
Of other fingers.
Then moved.
Palms rest on thighs,
Head is bowed, spine curved.

Another waiting room,
Another maudlin love song on the radio.
The singer sings a melody
As bland as the beige of the walls
As monotonous as the grey ceiling tiles.

'Happy birthday!' says the receptionist.
I share it with her daughter, two years my junior.
She tells me that this year she will gift money
Daughter and fiancé have a fresh mortgage, you see.
It's not easy for this generation to get ahead.
These concepts feel as far away as wellness.

Newly tired limbs on old tired limbs,
Layers of pain stacked on top
Of years of old pain.
My body interprets the loss that my mind could not
And my mind carries the weight of my body.

I close my eyes and time distorts.
The love song softens to a murmur.

'POETRY, THE INNER SELF AND LIVING WITH GRAVITY'

SOPHIE FINLAY

I suffer from postural orthostatic tachycardia syndrome (POTS), a disabling blood pressure disorder characterised by fainting, fatigue, tachycardia and perpetual dizziness. The cause of POTS is mysterious; somehow it originates in incorrect brain signals and results in a flawed response to the pull of gravity on the body's blood volume. My condition was triggered over six years ago and has left me partially disabled, hovering between upright posture and recumbency.

The difficulty of my life now remains – to what do I give my energy? For the chronically ill, energy is a precious commodity that must be managed precisely. How do I divide up the allotment of wellness? How do I fill the extensive periods of rest? However uncooperative my body has become, my mind and soul is filled with the same human need for thought and experience, for connection. Writing seems a natural space to express the restlessness of the cognitive and emotional energy locked in an often still body.

I have been a practising visual artist for many years. Since my illness I have turned my love of creating imagery inwards and started writing poetry. I have discovered the unique riches of this art: the internal imagery, the emotionality, the intricacies and the precisions of poetic expression. Poetry has become a joy and a solace I may not have otherwise fully explored.

I have written about fainting and about being bedridden. I have also researched historical experiences of illness. 'Diary from a Sanatorium: 1940s' is based on the actual diary of a woman suffering from tuberculosis.[27] Prior to the discovery of the antibiotic streptomycin, the treatment of tuberculosis was in many ways similar to the treatment of POTS: rest, pacing and gentle

....

27 The Royal Society of Medicine, 'Tuberculosis Sanatorium Regimen in the 1940s: a Patient's Personal Diary', *Journal of the Royal Society of Medicine*, vol. 97, no. 7, July 2004, pp. 350–3.

exercise therapy. It was a wonderful process to draw on both her voice and my own for this poem.

There is an absence of medical knowledge surrounding the cause of POTS; its complex mechanisms are buried inside the impenetrable prism of the automatic nervous system. Yet there is a strange sort of wisdom to this illness. It has forced me to slow down, to work part-time. It has put me out of step with the external world, but my inner world glows even more vividly. It has made my own soul translucent to me. Illness seems to bring about a curious dichotomy of experience – of struggle and solace, of loss and wisdom.

....

Syncope

Temporary loss of consciousness caused by low blood pressure.
From Greek 'syncope'; sun *'together'* + koptein *'strike, cut off'.*

Syncope
is to stop,
to cut off.

The pulling of blood
through the body's core,
like the spilling of self.

I have become
                liquid
and I walk like
                liquid,

spilling drowned movements.

Where have I gone?
In all this pool of my bed,

this collapsed and wall breached version of me.

Diary from a Sanatorium: 1940s

I suddenly coughed up mouthfuls of blood.
The dark liquid coagulates in my hand.
>   *Pulmonary Tuberculosis in the right lung.*
>   *Sanatorium for 9–12 months.*

After the first genuine rush of emotion,
other people are not interested in one's troubles.
I will keep it all inside of me, I will,
even though I will be separated from my baby.
He will reach bright milestones in the coming year.
I am determined not to be sad
when I see him forgetting me.

I'm getting used to the boarding school-cum-army atmosphere of the place,
and the language.
The different stages of rest:
>   'Absolute' is rest entirely in bed.
>   'Basins' is getting up to wash in own room.
Only talk in whispers.
>   'I'm on whispers' says a patient to me.
Whispers fall away into the air.
All that is unspoken and endured,
trailing off in whispers.

Strict routine and a constant stream of nurses.
Lights out at 9.30 pm.
I'm not allowed to talk about death.
Talk of death is folded
into the culture of rest and control.

But in the quiet whispers of the day
I remember dreaming of my white lungs.
White cavities nestle like vague ghosts
in the filmy opacity.

I dream of white shadows,
breathing in the ribs of my room.

Dysautonomia

The dream world looms
in the quiet tenor of my days.
I walk in green labyrinths,
tangled train tracks.

My sight shakes with each heartbeat
as the pulse of blood
traverses the long tract of my body.

Such quiet.
I am stripped to the core
where only pure thought remains,
and my sight.
I watch light move on the floor, the furniture,
a red flower down the street.
But there are sea-green tendrils in my heart.

Fainting is falling,
triggered by something buried deep, deep.
Something became activated,
an old voice.
It has pulled me down like a great hand.

Yet I have longed for peace, for slowness.
I want to watch trees gently change,
the weather, deep green shadows.
I want this communion
with the strange rivers of my interior.

'DISMANTLING THE ARMOUR'

RACHAEL MEAD

People who know me might be surprised to hear I have a chronic illness. I have spent years keeping it unspoken and hidden. Even after I was diagnosed with chronic depression and anxiety, I spoke about it only to a few trusted people and in ways that somehow distanced myself from it. I used medical terminology and spoke of symptoms and behaviours rather than how I felt. Suicidal ideation. Generalised anxiety disorder. Social phobia.

Eventually, writing became a natural fit; it suited my way of being in the world, participating, but from an analytical distance.

The taboo of mental illness is powerful. And like many who suffer from illnesses similar to mine, I tend to be hypersensitive and highly self-critical. In order to protect myself, I have an extroverted self that I show the world; it is a utilitarian mask and has become a default setting.

Until now, my writing has been another face of this mask, a performative self to protect me (and others from the perceived burden of me) in public. My poetry has always been an imaginative projection of my character rather than an exploration or revelation of my authentic self. In this way, my poetry has been another layer of armour. The rise of confessional poetry in the mid-twentieth century has aided me in this deception, as readers tend to unquestioningly accept that the 'I' is autobiographical.

In writing about my mental illness, I have revealed a hidden self. I have also revealed my choice to be unmedicated and the challenge of managing my illness day by day. It has been the most difficult writing I've ever done. These poems are raw and unworked because I feel they have been written by a different poet. A poet who is uncertain and unpractised. A poet who is emerging, in the most naked and painful sense.

What lies beneath my skin

The ringing phone ratchets me into tension.
It is everything and nothing,
filling the place poetry used to be.
Management only works in practice
and right now I'm all about theory.
The circling around guilt's drain.
The awareness of performance
– the inability to stop. The anger.
Everything turned inward.
I prefer silence and when I talk
it's all repetition. I let the phone ring.

Fear of death drops away like a silk dress
slipping from its hanger. The knife rack,
the rafters are pregnant with possibility.
I know what to do.
Walk the dog. Sometimes, this is all.
The gum trees raise their lacy fists,
a level of defiance I find impossible.
The glitter of creek water,
the black field of stars.
I put myself in the path of wildness
and let it fill my long and hollow bones.

At the psychologist

I pour it out, a glut of mud-purge.
One question and you are struggling
to catch this outpour of slumgullion,
a pressured stratigraphy of forty years
anger and emotion abruptly liquefied,
and just like that; biblical inundation.

But you catch it all, deftly, the tissues
placed just so, and you sift it down,
shaking out the last drops, easing it through
the mesh of questions, until we both sit there,
exhausted, looking down at what remains,
glittering on the dun face of the sieve.

....

Life on parole

I did my stretch in suburbia, hard labour
through the hormonal years, penned
behind corrugated fences, unscaleable
with the weight of family chained to my legs.
The yard was cross-hatched with the mesh
of shadow from the hills hoist, clothes hung
limp in their condemned shapes.
I waited out the years, the nights endured
with the knowledge that nowhere,
not even my own bunk was safe, a prison
with no lock on the bedroom door.
Through a window, I would see a woman
running, freedom bright on her face, flashing
in every stride and think   *one day, one day.*

I leapt down the first escape tunnel that opened under my feet
thinking this is freedom; transformation is death then rebirth.
But life on the outside was no fresh start, my convict past
etched across my skin like a homemade tattoo.
Metamorphosis, it seems, is the past and the present
writhing in same skin, the child still there

huddled in its damp puddle of dread, waiting
for the bedroom door to creak on its hinge.
Some days I'm only kept here by promises.
But every so often I put on my running shoes
and pushing hard I stride out from the long shadow
of the prison wall. Splitting open like a chrysalis my ribs
unfurl into bone-veined wings, my whole body loping,
breath shining its way through this bloody labyrinth,
no longer a prisoner of gravity, shackled to this earthen
ball of hard-packed stone – I am of the air.

'INHERITANCE'

GARETH ROI JONES

I grew up on a farm. Where physical labour like shearing, summer pruning, digging postholes or lifting twenty-foot-long sprinklers in the vineyard in the middle of summer heat were daily duties. Work that left you, at the end of the day, glad that it was the end of the day. With muscles sore and aching, and where a hot shower or, if lucky, a long soak in Epsom salts was the way to deal with it. A lot of this work involved repetitive bending over / standing up (summer pruning, rock picking, digging, lamb marking, etc.), the repeated nature of which often left me dizzy and with a thumping head even as a kid.

As with many things, my attitude to pain/relief is inherited from my parents.

1. *My father*: a farmer all his adult life and as reward for the hard labour of running a property, his body broke down, requiring surgery on knees, feet, spine, etc. For most of that time, he never complained. Just kept doing what (he thought) needed to be done; including one particularly memorable occasion where he was bowled over by an angry ram only a couple of weeks after one of his many knee surgeries. However, the more the years have caught up with him, the more extra-strength painkillers he has to take to cope. I inherited his attitude toward pain: as in, don't talk about it, don't acknowledge it, and maybe it'll go away. I didn't grumble (much); often didn't tell anyone when I was sore; just carried on because that's the way I'd seen it done – until one day I mentioned to my mother I'd had this really bad headache for three or four days (I've forgotten exactly how long because they were such constant occurrences).

2. *My mother*: a registered nurse, and while she's not quite a hypochondriac, she is very interested in the health and wellbeing of all those around her. She goes way beyond the usual 'eat a carrot' / 'put some sunscreen on', regularly checking that moles aren't becoming melanomas, questioning

the colour of phlegm and the consistency of stool, etc. All of this enhanced my reticence towards medicine and discussing health issues with her, partners, workmates, anyone. When I (perhaps foolishly, perhaps as a way of provoking action) mentioned my enduring headache, she immediately began an interrogation regarding the length/type/frequency/intensity/location of the pain before insisting I see a doctor or, at the very least, take some pain relief. I don't like being nagged and I don't like people poking around in my business; but given 'poking around' is pretty much what doctors do, the logical conclusion is: I don't like doctors. If I ever get a cold, I prefer curling up and riding it out rather than cluttering up a waiting room.

3. *Doctors*: I boarded for the first three years of my tertiary study, going back and forth to the farm in semester breaks and at the end of the academic year. When I finally began renting, I moved house about six times in seven years. This transience might be the reason I never really got an 'Adelaide doctor' – anything major, I would (and still do) drive back to the Valley to see one.

By this time, I'd been living with a seemingly never-ending headache for most of eternity. (I didn't even like using the word *migraines* because it seemed too much like 'complaining'; *headaches* seems smaller, more manageable.) But they were intensifying. I'd just moved house (an onerous chore which involved much packing, bending, standing, lifting, putting down of heavy boxes and boxes of books). So mum booked an appointment with the family GP and told me she expected me to attend. *Okay, I'll go – but don't expect me to enjoy it.* I didn't.

He began by saying I didn't seem to have been to the clinic in a while. *No. I live in town and don't go to doctors much.* Did I have a local doctor I saw in town? *No.* He seemed professionally offended by this. Auspicious beginning.

I told him about my symptoms and when I thought the headaches had come on. Mum's interrogation about the length/type/frequency/etc. of the pain came in handy. I mentioned the move. The boxes. That I'd experienced them in one form or another for years, but that the headaches seemed worse in the new house. Parts of the house had been freshly painted. Perhaps it was the fumes – but I'd gotten several killer ones even on days when the house had been wide open to fresh breezes blowing through every door and window.

Was it something I was eating or drinking? The internet lists a plethora of things that might cause 'migraines'. Some people have reactions to certain foods. Was I drinking too much alcohol (I know tannin in red wine gives a bigger mule's kick the older some people get; others are affected by the sulphites). But I went months without drinking and the headaches still flattened me. I made sure I drank enough water, wasn't dehydrated. Drank enough till it was leaking out my ears. No noticeable effect. Sugar, chocolate, caffeine, milk, ice cream: the list is almost endless. I went long periods abstaining from them all, one by one. Nada. Nothing seemed to help.

Was it the stress of a job I didn't enjoy? Well, the headaches kept coming, and with increasing intensity even twelve months after I'd resigned.

I noticed my biggest aches often coincided with times when I observed the water in the S-bend of the loo was low, sometimes the tide was almost half out (caused by a change in barometric pressure). I researched and discovered that, yes, there were some people whose migraines seemed to be set off by changes in the weather.

They seemed more common or of greater intensity whenever I came back from the farm to the city. Maybe I was allergic to suburbia. Or I just missed wide country vistas.

I told the doctor that one of the best moments writing a play is when the characters stop being 'forced along' by you, as writer, and begin talking by themselves and to each other independent of playwrighterly intervention. I joked: *my headaches feel like they're caused by characters from five different plays meeting at the pub and instead of just talking, they all shout.* The joke went over particularly well, and he did a couple of eye tests (checked out okay). Took my blood pressure. And said, 'Sometimes you can't explain these things'. Boom. Bulk bill please.

Fast forward three or four months. More complaining to mum. By this time I'd gotten over my dislike of taking medication (*it only masks the problem, doesn't cure it* had been my snooty attitude) because by God it helped, reducing it from 8's, 9's and 10's down to 3's and 4's – which by comparison felt fantastic. Except for those infrequent occasions when even half a dozen Panadeine Forte nicked from dad's medicine container did nothing.

So, I found myself back at the local clinic, but with a different GP this time. He seemed nicer, listened better, asked more questions, took some time with the eye chart. I think he took some blood or wanted me to have a blood test, I forget which exactly. Whenever it occurred, the results came back not showing signs of whatever he was looking for; I think diabetes was one trigger he mentioned.

I had an appointment in town where my head went through the big O of the CT machine. Obviously this is the one people worry about the most: a tumour on the brain. It too came back clean.

For a while, deteriorating eyesight was suspected as the key culprit. I saw an optometrist. First one since high school. Wow, had they changed in those intervening decades, but that's another conversation. Understandably, I'd lost a little vision (my parents laugh at how weak the magnification is in my glasses) but not enough to justify the extreme nature of the pain. I explained that I spend half my day staring at a screen, reading, reading, reading; and the other half buried in a book, reading, reading, reading – so my eyes did a fair bit of work. Eventually, glasses were acquired and although the severity and frequency lessened, the familiar phantom remained. It just became something I lived with.

For well over a year, I kept a record of what days the pain were on, what I was doing, how long it lasted and, when I could remember, what I'd eaten, how I'd slept, etc. – until I lost that notebook (which was particularly frustrating while writing this, as I kept wanting to consult it). One of the most difficult things about my ongoing internal war is that owing to the pain/state of my head, so much stuff is forgotten / blotted out by painkillers, naps, days spent going in and out of slumber.

There are still days which thump me. Knock me offcourse. It's been an interesting journey. As a writer I've long interrogated the thoughts that go on *inside* my brain, trying to understand them, what makes me tick. But this was a very different process. It was investigating the physical nature of what was happening *to* my brain. As I explained to mum recently, I feel my vocabulary to talk about the pain has expanded exponentially. I am now aware of and can articulate a range of pains, whereas before it just used to 'hurt'.

I now know that I have three main types of pain (in increasing order of severity):

i) slow burns, where my head aches, not at a level 8 or 9, just a steady grumbling 4, 5 or 6 that sort of hugs the outside of my whole skull.

ii) a slow stabbing pain that begins in my neck, or just above it, and creeps up to the right side of my head before staying there for as long as it feels necessary.

iii) a pounding, pulsating throb which makes my whole head feel like the speakers in a drum and bass club, like my brain is beating instead of my heart – thankfully this type of pain only lasts two to four hours.

One thing I've been 'lucky' with (I guess) is I've never needed to throw up (though I usually don't feel like eating much during these times; I make up for it later). Dizziness is common, usually accompanying a couple of headaches a month. Sometimes my vision gets blurry or lights seem to flash in front of my eyes. Sometimes too, my whole body tingles. I have become inordinately fond of dark, quiet rooms. I'm better at working through them, better at taking something to relieve the agony, better at talking about them.

But what causes them? My personal theory, for what it's worth, is the worst ones come with extreme or rapid meteorological changes. Whether this is true, or I've just tricked myself into thinking this way, I really don't know anymore. In a way it doesn't much matter. This is what I live with, my genetic inheritance and, for better or worse, it's a part of what makes me, me.

the paddock

on the road into town
our redneck neighbours
have a barren grassless
perennially overstocked
livestock paddock
dad & his mates only
half-jokingly call
the *linger & die paddock*

where there's always
at least half a dozen
extremely unwell sheep
blighting the hillsides
with their lethargic
wanderings before
giving up & becoming
another bloated carcass

sometimes my brain
grazes there too

poltergeist

he almost doesn't notice the dull ache
so long has its ghost haunted him

except, say:

– if the barometric pressure changes wildly
     the ghost howls like a wolf pack
– if he has one glass of wine too many
     the ghost punches bone
– if the pollen count rises
     the ghost sneezes cannonballs
– if he bends down & up too often
     the ghost knocks books from shelves
– even if he stands too swiftly
     the ghost shouts about everything, anything

he says it's like having a well-dressed
proselytising religious spectre
standing on the mat, knock-knocking
on his front door, all day, every day
even though he never lets him in
still he stands there knock-knocking
sometimes gently,
        but some days
the spirit splits in two, like the broom
of the sorcerer's apprentice, then each
of those, two again, & again, & again
till they're clamouring all round
the house knock-knocking, knock
-knocking & no door in the world
can keep the wraiths away

aching

afternoons are a succession
of micro naps because it's easier
than being awake

hours when simply standing up
is a pickaxe

when the growling dog
won't let you through the gate

lose days in the swell
counting down minutes
till you can swallow
the next little ball of relief

no memories of meeting people
nor the things said

not understanding why the universe
is pushing everything in when all
you want is to let *anything* out

a nihilist wandering wasteland
where the end seems easier
than the going on

'FORGETTING MY SELF'

STEVE EVANS

I was ten years old and confined to bed with a mild fever and bad headache. The rain drummed on the window next to me. I badly wanted to go to sleep and wake refreshed, without the clamminess and without the maddening sensitivity to noise and light. I began to feel that I was not only floating up and down but also simultaneously shrinking and then reverting to my normal size. The effect was literally dizzying but fascinating.

Such occasions of feeling untethered and weightless, together with Alice in Wonderland–like properties of size-changing, did recur. Later I discovered that this state is sometimes associated with migraines, and the coming years would have me suffer a number of those. They diminished over the years, however. I went from having one severe episode every couple of months to perhaps one or two a year.

We cannot think of everything we are exposed to in any given instant of living. That would be nonsensical. The brain necessarily filters information into levels of attention and, hopefully, still allows us to focus most on what really matters at the time. Is that car running a red light? Am I in danger? Do I need to buy more milk?

What we don't realise is that our brain also skips information. It can jump little puddles of experience so small that we don't know that it's happening, and yet we believe we are functioning normally because we are unaware of it. That is how my neurologist explained things after I finally had MRI scans to get to the bottom of some worrying cognitive events. Looking at a scan of my brain, he pointed out tiny dots that represented scars, the signs of moments when it was briefly injured without me knowing. There were times, though, when I did know – during or, more worryingly, afterwards.

One day as I painted a bathroom ceiling, I realised that I could not think of the name of any of the eight or nine family members who were in my house at the time. I told my wife to keep an eye on me (at least I knew we were a couple) and the effect soon passed. Months later as I walked down the steps of a lecture theatre holding some notes, I could not recall who

I was or why I was there, though logic said I must be a university lecturer and about to give a lecture – which I did, gradually remembering that I had prepared the material and gaining a sense of ownership. Most worrying was the day I drove from work, collected my children at school, and was almost home before I realised what I was doing, that I was not still sitting at my work desk.

These experiences are captured in one of the poems, as are aspects of the medication's side effects. My left-lobe epilepsy relates to memory, unlike the right-lobe sited variety. It has proved treatable and is still in check, as far as I can tell.

Some things have changed for the worse. My motor skills are not as good as before. At times, I find my walking is less steady. I would also like to have my old fluid style of handwriting back but that is not such a big matter. I could do without the periods of tiredness produced by the drugs, as they are limiting. There are days when I feel my thinking is not as sharp as I would like, but who is to know what underlying cause is to blame? I suspect it is due to the drugs and I am aware when my level of creative activity drops away. For someone who writes poetry, fiction and nonfiction, this is a concern.

On balance though, and at least to this point, I think I have been lucky. I function pretty much as I used to, albeit with an attached ritual of seeing medical practitioners plus purchasing and taking the medication. I began by mentioning migraines. It appears that those with epilepsy often reveal a history of such headaches, although the reverse is not strongly connected. What that means is unclear.

My life changed. I know very keenly that many people have to deal with much worse than me, and I am grateful for what I have. This life is still a Wonderland, even if I am nothing like Alice.

....
Diagnosis

The scans he holds to a square of light
Show pretty scars.
He asks about the episodes.
Names sometimes remote as stars, I say,
Even my own family's.
I tell him of the stranger's talk I gave
Buying time until the notes I held
Had slowly turned to mine.
But worst was driving the children home
While thinking I was at my desk.

I'm an unwilling time traveller,
A tune with holes in it
Sounding like music that no one plays,
But music all the same.
Gradual erasure is someone else's game.
This is just a visiting absence,
An erratic striptease backwards and forwards
That undoes me from the present
Then slips me back inside again.

It's left-lobe epilepsy he says drugs can fix
But no more driving.
Ahead are years of this little buzz
At the back of my skull
To reassure me I am almost here.
A performance poem
And always a work in progress.
I wonder how to break the news.

Valproate

Time tripped and split,
And spat me out
Into another time.
I did get my old present back,
Though at a cost.
Some parts better, others worse.
The medicine I'm now prescribed
Is partly blessing, partly curse.
The side effects are numerous.

The ring of constant tinnitus.
Headaches for days;
I'd sleep right through them if allowed,
Emerging clear at the other end.
Instead, I drowse the dizzy hours
Where balance has lost interest,
Leaves me swooning at the world
Like an astronaut adrift,
Walking tipsy while playing sober,
Fighting the sway of corridors.

I'm in a haze.
Beyond the physical malaise.
More fractures in the self I was,
With mood swings I try to suppress.
I ride their waves but cannot swim.
No god or science has the cure.
The hum of my new universe
Turns out to be a hiss.
I'm not the same, but no one is.

The Body Electric

My body is short-circuiting.
Handwriting jitters through
The weak link between thought and deed.
But still I cannot sing it right.
Even if I go quite slow there are
Glitches in transmission,
Triggers keep sparking tiny fits,
Bursts of static that translate
Into strings of senseless code.
The tremors take over.
I'm disconnected.

Once the cursives flowed with ease.
Now the lines are drawing me
Staccato, in jerks and twitches,
Barbed wire strung across a page.
The unexpected flicks are itches
That I cannot scratch,
Unplanned excursions I try to fight
With cramped miniatures,
Letters held tight to the memory
Of how I used to write.
As those stitches spring apart,
I see the poor machine I am.

There are tablets for this, true,
Although they do not always work.
Once fluid strokes succumb to hooks
And sudden jagged tangles.
Shopping lists grow alien shapes.
Jotted messages fake Sanskrit.
Flourishes of elegance disintegrate
And my words are brittle copies
Of what I used to do. My fingers fail.
I just can't make a fist of this.

'THE POLITICS OF FRAGILITY:
DISABILITY AND SHAME'

SUSAN HAWTHORNE

Epilepsy is an ancient word and comes from the Greek word to seize or attack: *epilambanein*. It is, in a way, a seizing of the self. In the case of tonic-clonic seizures (called 'grand mal' for many years) the self utterly disappears, and depending on the severity of the seizure the person can be out of it for ten minutes to many hours. It can then take a day or two to really get back on your feet. (Although I have been known to give a paper at a conference two hours later.)

I heard the word 'epilepsy' for the first time as an adolescent. My mother had insisted I read an article about it in *Life* magazine, though I already knew that shame was attached to this illness. I knew it because I was told to say that the pills I took were to 'stop me from getting over-excited' and I knew that the taking of these pills marked me as different. As a child, I wasn't terribly curious because I had no memories of seizures, which had been fairly infrequent. This was to change in my twenties when, after a long period of being seizure free, they resumed.

This propelled me to find out more, look at the medical research and think about the potential long-term side effects of my medication. The decisions I made then have, I believe, contributed to my good health.

Shame and fear are two elements that hover around epilepsy and I have wondered for a long time about why this is. The fear is understandable. When a person dies, often a seizure is the last obvious manifestation of the dying body. So seizures are associated with death. When a person has a seizure and recovers, it has frequently been associated with returning from the dead. The moniker 'the sacred disease' is probably connected to this understanding that the person has visited the place of the gods.

Shame is harder to understand, but I suspect that shame comes from the lack of control a person has over her/his body in a seizure. The body might vomit, urinate or excrete in public as well as enter a state of unconsciousness and therefore have no recall of these events. I understand from friends that being present at a seizure is a no-fun experience. Knowing this, however, I cannot experience it as they have. It can cause people to throw a bucket of water over the body and call an ambulance unnecessarily; it can result in name-calling by children and worse.

I am one of the lucky ones because I have had relatively few seizures in my life, but each time brings a new insight. At twenty I gained a sense of my mortality and it made me aware that my life could be cut short at any time without warning. So live for the day. I am aware of the fragility of existence and that the universe does not care. I try therefore to live well, to be attentive to others because you never know what is going on behind a person's face. Epilepsy is an invisible disability, except for when it isn't, and then it can be flamboyantly and spectacularly visible.

....
Eurydice

Orpheus sings as he returns
from the dead.

Eurydice cried out, *Don't
leave me here like this.*

Eurydice's eyes are dry
with fear and anger

As darkness closes in on her
once again.

descent

the call
that hollow sound of Cumaea
I was here before
thousands of years ago

your hundred mouths
shouting
words frothed at the edge
of my mouth

the journey looming
flight into the unknown
descent into
the dark thighs of your cave

my hair snake-wreathed
Etruscan Medusa
speaking with a hundred voices
the sibilant hiss of prophecy

seizure grasped
she flails at vanishing memory
bruised she rises from darkness
almost misses the plane

....

someone's fear

a seizure in a room filled with couches
who called the ambulance?

a few minutes of unconsciousness
someone's fear calls the ambulance

by the time they arrive she is talking
she walks out to the ambulance

she says I don't need an ambulance
someone's fear called the ambulance

when the $1600 ambulance bill arrives
someone's fear is not around to pay

'SIT THE PAIN AWAY'[28]

STUART BARNES

'It is amazing how much my "sits" help...I begin to understand what
T. S. Eliot means in "Ash Wednesday": "Teach us to care and not to care."'
– *Christopher Isherwood,* Diaries: Volume One, 1939–1960

In 2014 a GP diagnosed a bulging disc. He theorised that my L4-L5 had been damaged when I was date raped in 1996. He insisted on surgery – a spinal fusion – so I found another sensible GP, who confirmed the bulging disc and my suspicion of sciatica in the right leg. He prescribed Endone and referred me to a physiotherapist.

For many years I had not sought rehabilitation; the touch of a partner at the small of my back, where my rapist had punched me repeatedly, triggered flashbacks so I especially feared the hands of a male physiotherapist, the disturbance I knew his hands would surface. So my first was a woman. Eventually, scheduling meant I had to see a man. I wasn't ready to, but my muscles and nerves still felt as if they were being twisted and burnt by a ghastly, invisible master puppeteer.

Several months later, a friend recommended a male acupuncturist. I didn't hesitate to make an appointment. Like my GP and physiotherapists, he encouraged me to meditate daily, which was initially difficult (for support, I used one of my Queenslander walls), but my back's muscles strengthened quickly and soon I could do my 'sits' without assistance. His needles, moxa, tuning forks, cups and herbs continue to aid my recovery.

Living with these conditions can be frustrating: I wake to pain, which has to be managed throughout the day; I can't always write and edit when I would like to; I have had to stop attending yoga class; I can no longer push a petrol

....
28 A transformation of Peaches' 'Fuck the Pain Away'.

or electric mower; sometimes I need to rest when I would rather be spending time with friends; I have gained weight; sex can be arduous. But I'm grateful for what I've learnt: to meditate on waking, in the afternoon and before sleep (I won't write in detail about my meditations except to say they're the best sort of pain relief); that when it comes to Endone, less is more; to perform my physiotherapy exercises regularly; to exercise differently, i.e. to walk and cycle, do yoga at home (swimming was exacerbating pain).

Last year I started wearing orthotics – immediately life-changing.

Last year, too, alone in the bush, I narrated my rape. My bulging disc throbbed, my leg twitched. I almost fell over when I had finished; I was that naturally high (my 'trip' continued well into the night). A deep sleep. On waking, I realised that I had affixed my rape to 1996; it would no longer lumber amorphously, razing confidence, trust and love. Now, sex is without terror, and the pain in my spine and leg has diminished significantly.

Writing much of my earlier poetry, which explored psychology, psychiatry and trauma, often generated anxiety and depression. Recording pain is new and energy-giving. It balances the scales – it distances me from my mind and draws me towards my body. It inflates my body as I inflate my diaphragm during meditation or yoga.

My poem 'Cups' was written after an early acupuncture appointment. 'Ari' – the name of my rapist, Hebrew for lion – emerged after a morning meditation. This poem was difficult to transcribe, and can be difficult to read – the language of 'sits' is erratic. I enjoy subverting medical documents –'ENDONE® Oxycodone hydrochloride 5 mg' is a remix of some of the text from Endone oxycodone hydrochloride CMI.[29]

....

29 myDr, ENDONE® oxycodone hydrochloride, *myDr Consumer Medicine Information*, www.mydr.com.au/medicines/cmis/endone-tablets.

Cups

after Gwen Harwood

I know them by their lips. I know the proverb
about immediacy. Many slip
and shatter on sheer concrete, the older, the glass.
They held the common cold in hieratic,

are octopus-suckers. I imagine them
thus, lying facedown on acupuncture tables.
I apprehend firebirds. Their fearsome vacuum
surfaces disturbance. Flying saucers

might inscribe similar discs of stillness
in cereal: formations of purple, rose:
thirteen moons, an earth, a sun in syzygy.
They order qi, are venerable remedy.

They never play hard to get. Foul deed, foul day they aren't.
All bell, no whistle. Anti-insurrection.
A trance in sudsy buckets; rinsed, their lips
await others' blue skin. Love, their love is blind.

....

Ari

The tulips should be behind bars like dangerous animals;
They are opening like the mouth of some great African cat.
– Sylvia Plath, 'Tulips'

        morning, I dew
-claw visions of queens
          the Queen
-slander opens like
      the mouth of some
    great African
cat   the empurpled
    dimpled tongue unfur
-ls   Surya Namaskara
I sw   -allow my tail in Cobra

    a dangerous past
      life animals a fu
          -ture like tulips

      cross-legged on
  Solomon's   carpet
      sit   bones sink

      at each in
      -halation
          I spin
      white
  light int

-o   gold

    seeks the
  lumbar pulse

        a sulphur
      crested cockat

-oo's   prehist
    -orical
looking beak sh
-redding a sky of
     calico can't
sever
    this Nirvana

....

ENDONE® Oxycodone hydrochloride 5 mg*

Blister-white tablet engraved with 'ENDONE'
on one side, break bar the other.
It does not take the place of your doctor
or pharmacist: opium or morphine:
Accident or Emergency.

Store it below ground, above ground, in
an unlocked cupboard. Store it in the bathroom,
store it near the sink. Leave it on every
window sill, leave it in the car. Swallow
it before meals with a glass of nausea.

Do not show your pupils, abnormal,
do not show your restlessness, do not show your goose
-flesh, do not show your fast heart rate, do not show your new
-born child to a doctor or pharmacist.

*Note: A found poem; myDr, ENDONE® oxycodone hydrochloride, *myDr Consumer Medicine Information*, www.mydr.com.au/medicines/cmis/endone-tablets.

'BENEATH THE SKIN'

IAN GIBBINS

Due to a combination of good luck and deliberate lifestyle decisions to minimise risk of conditions that have affected my immediate family members, I am fortunate not to have acquired any chronic illnesses. As in any family, many members of mine do experience chronic disease: metabolic (including cardiovascular, endocrine and autoimmune conditions), unresolved visceral pain and lifelong mental conditions. And then there are the consequences of surgery for cancer or other life-threatening conditions, and the insidious signs of ageing as it affects body and mind to varying degrees. But this is not what I have written about here.

For thirty years, twenty of them as Professor of Anatomy, I taught the structure and function of the human body to students in medicine, health sciences and engineering. In different contexts and using diverse teaching methods, we explored the intricate details of how the body works under normal circumstances, how it deals with abnormal conditions of disease and injury, and what happens when it eventually fails. Most of my classes focused on the way we move: the complex mechanical interactions between muscles and bones; the interplay between airways and the cardiovascular system that keeps the body going; and how the brain underpins absolutely everything we do, or even think about doing. We explored the full scale of knowledge from the molecular level to the social interactions of individuals.

In addition to teaching, I ran an active laboratory-based research program as a neuroscientist, investigating the microscopic organisation of the nerves that communicate between the internal organs and the spinal cord. Some of these nerves control the activity of the organs, while others monitor such activity and report back to the rest of the nervous system. If there is dysfunction, injury, or inflammation of the internal organs, stimulation of these sensory nerves underlies the experience of pain. My research, along with that of my collaborators and colleagues locally, interstate, and around the world, revealed the amazing complexity and sophistication of these signalling pathways.

As a result of my teaching and research, I was privileged to acquire a deep understanding of the unseen phenomena occurring within the body, beneath the skin, beyond the limits of unaided perception. How, then, to explain what it feels like when the body does not perform as expected, when injury or infection or inherited abnormality, perhaps in just a single gene or protein sequence, undermines our reassuring assumption that the body will simply keep on going, at least for the foreseeable future? What images can we conjure up to illustrate to others the internal breakdowns, the disruption of perception, the distortion of interaction with the known and unknown worlds we inhabit? Perhaps this is where poetry can help.

Language, and the way we use it, is one of the key biological qualities that makes us human. As marvellous as it is, however, language fails us all too often, especially when we are faced with deep emotion, raw physical experience, unfamiliarity with a world for which we have no words and no shared vocabulary. Poetry, perhaps more than any other art form, can attempt to fill this void by putting into words that for which words do not exist. So, the three poems presented here build on my experiences as a teacher, researcher and poet to imagine, enliven and report the unspoken, perhaps the unspeakable, the feelings, the confusion and disbelief, together with subsequent meaning-making that accompany life lived through a dysfunctional body.

'Cataplexy' is a rare neurological condition in which extremes of emotion lead to a sudden, but brief, switch from normal consciousness into a waking dream-like state with loss of muscle tone. It is probably caused by a single mutation in a specific neurotransmitter system within the hypothalamus.

'Paraplegia' considers the loss of lower body function, including control of some internal organs, here as a result of a childhood spinal injury, maybe caused by a car accident, and the subsequent oscillations between acceptance and rejection, between dreams of something better and simply something else.

'Sometimes it Hurts': more than 25 per cent of women experience genital pain at some point in their lives, but for a proportion of them, it is always present, often at levels that not only preclude normal sexual function, but also restrict a range of daily activities. Female genital pain was the focus on one of the last research projects I was involved in, and the poem is informed by case reports of women with this condition.

Sometimes it hurts

When you come to me
I feel your heat before your touch,
I feel the wind, hot, from a midsummer
night, prickling with dried leaves,
endlessly irritable crickets, incipient thirst,
with the inevitable sunrise that follows,
that, in this climate of ill-defined seasons,
threatens fire before our first morning breath.

When you come to me,
I shiver like a violin string;
in cold sweat, my lip glistens with
dew-drops, my skin draws tight, tighter,
constricts my arteries and veins, a thunderbolt
blinds my shadows, ghostly spectres haunt
my path, sing storm-wracked sirens' songs,
disguise ancient fog-bound shipping hazards.

When you come to me,
I count all the stars across the sky,
the sand grains on the beach, in the desert,
the heartbeats I always lose, the pangs
I fear as your caresses slip unguided
into the voids of boundless space, as each
and nearly every one of your kisses falls
into unacknowledged whispers around me.

Paraplegia

[1]
In the absence of speech, I could only touch
and grasp and hold: I did not know there were
bees in the air, hairy caterpillars in the grass,
unless I itched, scratched, turned my skin red,
wished my mother to bathe me with milk and
sea-shanties, with cotton so soft I grew invisible;

unwilling to walk, I was not troubled by gravel
tearing my shoes, black cats treading my path,
where I should place my feet, my hips, my knees
during the progressive waltz or cha-cha-cha;
earth tremors gave me little pause for thought,
irreparable ligaments never slowed my progress;

before I understood the nature of dreams,
the distinction between rise and fade, stupor
and illusionary wakefulness, I too often confused
an atmosphere of suspense with misting sky glow,
tessellated by elms, poplars, sprawling oaks,
defied flight and leaden stall, and then, and then,

[2]
and then I had a tail like a horse, like Pegasus,
a life reborn preternaturally, transitional,
suffused by discovery, a phantasm of adventure,
the elusive who-cares-what-will-happen-next,
the what-the-hell-derring-do that ignites
sparks in your eyes, lightning conductors
in your steps, that leaves your apprehension
spread-eagled, dielectric, at the tips of my wings,

and then darkness unspoken, nothing to say,
with wheel-rims over-tightened, barely capable
of marking the flagstones, so she, so I screamed

and insects fell from the ceiling, swarmed
a boulevard in Portugal or France, after we failed
to catch the word for home, when misaligned,
no longer punch-drunk, we lay thread-stripped,
unable to stand beneath our paralysis of future;

[**3**]
and now the beast on my back, canines, carnassials
grinding in my ear, hackles laid low, relaxes its
ictal grip, retracts eight harpoon claws, bequeaths
another hour to prepare our stealthy departure;

cast adrift, I feint escape, chart perilous diversions
from meandering creek-bed to deep oceanic plains,
past dry Marram dunes and petrified wood, through
the untainted dead weight of incoming abyss;

a looming tally of roadside cairns, scribed with
ravelled skeins of lichen, a-fleck with wind-worn
reminiscence, the mementoes abandoned by one
last journey beyond our aching conviviality;

until the sleep, the sleep you always promise,
embraces my icy rigor, fills my breast with incense,
lifts me so high you see me shimmer and float,
luminous as a glory above your faltering sun.

Cataplexy

or in the garden eyes your eyes buttons :
on the ground and my shirt sodden :
shrink-wrapped around my torso my waist hips :
and buttons undone missing on the ground :
or maybe frogs giant toads eels that slither :
entwine my ankles left leg right and :

arrive with skeins hanks our bowlines the restaurant :
with tagliatelle in ink indecisive then roulade then sabayon :
again with sangiovese sparkling the heat until you laughed :
you said your :

map in my pocket with copper coins a docket :
my hands too deep too far from polar co-ordinates :
a falling star but now only jelly-jam and cake :
birthday candles when my grandmother an owl :
under the eaves sings coos for the moon to wax and wane :
the television static the television the television :

at the gate two dollars or one hundred or never sufficient :
bricks falling a falling star dust matting our hair :
lightning between our watch dials so we run and run :
so flares sparkling between our radios our telephones :
disconnected the cavernous space of :

phosphogenic the haze any longer did you ?
look into the setting sun driving drive me home mistyped :
the cavernous emptiness of did you read the headlines did ?

knees elbows in alluvial mud clay buttons blue buttons my shirt :

did you look into the sun ?

passionfruit sabayon or not :

candles alight is the snow you promised ?

or not did you ?

frogs and eels beyond my grasp your touch entangle :
receding still sodden so :

buttons blue buttons white and my hands are empty :
skin bare against :

driving away :

when we kiss an owl a blackbird somewhere :
near the homeward road golden braids and knots I cannot :
he you sleepless untied or else tadpoles giant toads :
cramp in your calves or else :

falling as now and now now altogether soundless :
what happens when tongue-tied this shoulder :
pain in the small of my back did you see you ?

or yesterday thereabouts the watch face the dial at a glance :
mistaken absolutely nothing buttons your buttons :
your blue buttons and I ask about the sky and the rain :
and lightning sparkles time undetermined sodden falling :

and you laugh laughter in the garden entwined around me :
or not and all your friends are looking at :

'INHERITED PAIN'

MEG DUNLEY

My life of chronic pain was determined long before I was born. I come from a family of migraineurs. Often Mum came home from work, head in hands, retreating to her bedroom for hours. On Fridays Dad came home from work, popped a couple of Mogadon and passed out. Nor was my older brother spared. At university, he was regularly knocked out with a migraine (an hour after arriving for lectures, which was also about half an hour after consuming a Mars Bar and a packet of Twisties).

My migraines snuck up on me. It's difficult to remember at what age I started getting them or when the pain was particularly noticeable. But I recall when I was about ten or eleven, the family had gone out for yum cha. It was a delightful experience, until I hopped in the car to come home and was struck with intense pain and nausea. Now, I put that down to a possible allergy to MSG – not uncommon with migraine sufferers. Weekly trips to the library were marred when, after a good hour reading, I was again felled by nausea during the drive home. When Dad noticed the large amount of Panadol being consumed, I had to accept I had a problem and confessed to being the Panadol thief.

Fast-forward another five years, I looked for any cause for the now-daily migraines. One doctor suggested I had sinus pain and recommended an ear, nose and throat specialist. The specialist shook his head and delivered the grave news: *just* migraines located in the sinus.

Twenty-five years on from there, and thirty-five years from the MSG incident, I have tried numerous preventative medications that have all failed in the end.

One of the worst experiences was when I was knocked out with tranquillisers in hospital for five days in an attempt by the neurologist to 'trick' my brain into forgetting the entrenched migraine memory. My head continued to ache, even though I had lost all feeling through the inside of my mouth, throat and nose, and the neurologist walked away saying there was nothing else he could do.

Now I subject myself to twelve weekly doses of thirty-one ridiculously painful injections of Botox (I still can't fathom that people do this for beauty). But Botox alone isn't enough, so I also take additional preventative medications, use myriad alternative therapies (none of which are proven to help) and still suffer eighteen migraines a month on average.

For a couple of reasons, it's not something I tell people when I meet them. The first is that people generally cannot conceive of the idea of waking most days with a migraine, and they want to know how I get on with life (I do because I have to). The second reason is the list of remedies that they recommend. I will often be given a shopping list of ideas – most of which I have tried already (except for the latest fad: piercing of the ear cartilage). One of the more abstract treatments suggested was masturbation.

There are only a handful of people I know who can pick that I have a migraine when they see me. 'You've got one?' they say. Apparently there's a look in my eyes when I have one. One friend can pick when I'm about to get one – long before me.

Time has helped with managing this chronic illness. I have learned to pick up the early signs (irritation, restlessness, heightened senses) and therefore treat myself. I have also learned to have patience with pain. Pain doesn't like impatience and will dig its bony heels in and set up residence. My approach to treatment has vastly improved from the early days. I know which drugs will offer immediate relief, but which will encourage the migraine to swing back with a vicious punch four hours later. I avoid most of my triggers (food, noise, light, alcohol, exercise, stress) to varying degrees according to how close I am to the edge.

I am better at managing my life around the chronic pain. I work part-time, study and manage a busy family with three teenage boys. I smile and remind myself that if it gets too bad I can lie down.

Sadly, I have passed the dysfunctional gene onto one of my sons. My hope for him is that the migraines never reach the chronic stage of my own and that research will shed light on better treatment and prevention.

....

Yes, is the lie

My brain is broken / that's how it feels
But there's no glue to fix it / only time and more time
Piles of pills / popped from their shells
Handfuls thrown down / tired throat accepts.

You better yet? / is the endless question
Yes, is the lie.

I croak like a smoker / it's like having a stroke
Doc's only answer / scribbles a script
waves of strokes wake me / each day like a child
Needy, oh so needy / I've nothing to give.

Squeeze my eyes shut / insistence keeps on
I peel off the bed / and limp up the hall
Squint in the dark / more pills: blue, white and yellow
Lie in wait for that moment / relief, then sleep.

You better yet?
Yes.

Frozen

Five minutes in the chair / twelve weeks of frozen
Poison under my skin / thirty-one shots of Botox
No beauty in chronic pain

Friends stare, look for change / can't tell, they say
hoping they could / shame he doesn't slip, they say
I can't raise an eyebrow

My reflection stares back / I smile hard
try to raise an eyebrow / plastic forehead shines back
Who am I looking at?

A jab in the ribs / lucky you, they say
I smile, laugh, mask the truth / can't tell them
No luck in chronic pain

Have you tried?

Have you tried some
Yoga
Pilates
Acupuncture
A hypnotist
A naturopath?

What about a little
Meditation
Relaxation
Music therapy
Aromatherapy
A massage at all?

What about
Some walking
Or swimming
Tried weights
Or tai chi?

I've heard
Feverfew
Evening Primrose
Coenzyme Q10
B12 and Folic are good.

Then there's a
Chiropractor
Physio or Osteo
Maybe a
Myotherapist
Maybe a Quack?

Isagenix
A diet
No dairy

No protein
No carbs or meat
A fast?

No caffeine
No grog
No soft drinks
No citrus
Are you drinking
Enough water?

I s'pose you've tried everything
but you never know
don't know if you don't try
I'll send you the link.

'BODIES OF "I" AND THE UNCERTAINTY OF POETRY'

HEATHER TAYLOR JOHNSON

When I was first diagnosed with Ménière's disease my doctor was all about numbers: frequency of full-blown attacks when the world around me spins violently for hours; vertigo levels on days between the full-blown attacks; percentages of hearing loss according to the tests administered earlier that day. Never mind that I'd only been living in Australia for a little more than a year while my family and friends remained scattered throughout the United States. Never mind that I'd had to stop skydiving, something I'd been doing for eight years with enormous passion, something that contributed to my self-identity, something that provided me with community. Never mind that I was trying to do a master's degree while coping, barely, day to day. None of those things could be graphed. Those things didn't count.

With each medical appointment I tried to explain what vertigo felt like for me because I wanted to talk to someone who had knowledge of the illness. I naively thought we could learn from one another and I craved an empathetic smile. But he'd turn the conversation around and bring it back to numbers: 'So when was your last Ménière's attack?' (Insert date; did it really matter?)

I was sick, and I'm talking about two bodies when I say 'I'.[30] The *corporal body* is a body of mass, an (ill-)functioning body; the *lived body* is an experience-rich body, that which dreams, that which frets and cries. I bring these two bodies together when I speak about 'I' – such an obvious thing; to me it seems inevitable. But my doctor didn't do that, leaning biasedly toward the corporal.

In the isolation of my quiet room I was desperate to write poems that

....

30 Adapted from V. Kalitzus's discussion of 'Körper' and 'Leib' in 'Life "In Limbo": Donor Families, Organ Recipients and their Experience in Germany', in P. L. Twohig and V. Kalitzkus (eds), *Making Sense of Health, Illness and Disease*, Amsterdam: Rodopi, 2004, p. 305.

would describe my corporal body in chaos and make sense of that chaos by shaping it around narratives of my lived body. When I tried, all I got was anger, self-pity, desperation. Lines through words, Xs through lines, dreaded exclamation points. At twenty-five, I felt like a fourteen-year-old girl writing crappy poetry of woe-is-me, *alas! alas!*, drawing on images of a single teardrop. What I needed was comfort through words and my own were working against me. I grew depressed. *If not my words, then whose?*

Where could poetry of the ill be found? Not in any self-help books on coping with illness. Not in any pamphlets in the waiting room of my doctor's office or in any Google searches from my home computer. I liken my need at the time to what Audre Lorde said of Angelina Weld Grimké, a Harlem Renaissance poet who never identified as a Black Lesbian:

> I often think of [her] dying alone in an apartment in New York City in 1958 while I was a young Black Lesbian struggling in isolation at Hunter College, and I think of what it could have meant in terms of sisterhood and survival for each one of us to [have] known of the other's existence: for me to have had her words and her wisdom, and for her to have known I needed them! It is so crucial for each one of us to know she is not alone.[31]

I craved this too: poetry of solace and recognition.

Frustrated enough to denounce my would-be-poet status, I turned to prose, wrote a novel and gave my ageing male protagonist the disease.[32] I felt liberated, in a sense and for a time, but I found that I wanted to keep writing about my illness, the corporal and the lived body together, the 'I' that I had become and was becoming. The aching need to communicate was as chronic as the illness itself, and because each new bout of Ménière's brought with it new pain and new insight, there would have to be new poems.

But the poetry pulled me in directions that frightened me, making me admit to the failure of my corporal body and forcing me to accept the anxiety compacting in my lived body. A writer, in my experience, is a heady mixture of insecurity and ambition, so while I hated the poems I wrote on illness, I was determined to keep on writing them until I got them right, until I was

....

31 A. Lorde, 'A Burst of Light', *A Burst of Light: Essays by Audre Lorde*, Ithica, New York: Firebrand Books, 1988, pp. 117–18.
32 H. Taylor Johnson, *Pursuing Love and Death*, Sydney: Harper Collins, 2013.

confident enough to try for publication and not cringe if someone accepted my work.

Eventually, someone did. I don't know if those poems were right. I don't know if these poems are right. I don't know what right is, exactly, and I certainly don't know if I'll ever get a poem of illness right. Words fail the body. Words fail trauma. Virginia Woolf wrote about their ineptitude in her essay 'On Being Ill'.[33] Susan Sontag warned us against the use of metaphors in *Illness as Metaphor*[34] – metaphor: a poet's best friend. Writers who've suffered serious illness know this struggle, have meditated on it, obsessed over it, and at this point in my writing, at this point in my illness, I am one more.

....

33 V. Woolfe, 'On Being Ill', *Collected Essays: Volume IV*, London: The Hogarth Press, 1967, pp. 193–203.

34 S. Sontag, *Illness as Metaphor and AIDS and its Metaphors*, London: Penguin, 1991.

Trying to Talk about Ménière's Disease

1.

It's been a long time since you've been to the doctor. The last one laughed when you told him acupuncture keeps your illness at bay. 'You know it's unpredictable.' Ménière's disease is unpredictable; you've always known this because, in fact, you live with it. He says, 'Maybe it just hasn't come back because it's unpredictable.' Maybe it hasn't come back because it's unpredictable. 'And don't forget you've been having babies.' How could you ever forget that? There are three of them. The oldest one knows where you keep the needles and Stemetil. 'Pregnancy does funny things to the body.' Yes, you have to admit that pregnancy did do funny things to your body. It made your bladder feel fuller faster. It made your feet and back ache if you stood for more than seven minutes. Pregnancy made your stomach huge. 'It's highly likely it's not the acupuncture.' And then he laughed, as if something was funny. You found nothing to be funny at all.

Without voice, boulders
speak with their bodies, loudly,
then sit in silence.

2.

It's been a long time since you've been to the doctor. They always say there is nothing they can do, so what has ever been the point? There is no treatment; there is no cure. There is a surgical procedure that might cause you to go deaf in your bad ear while you anticipate the return of it in your good one, but acupuncture keeps the illness at bay; still, you need to talk about new discoveries, maybe there are new drugs for the very worst days when you cannot get out of bed to get to your acupuncturist. And there aren't new discoveries, or drugs, but he wants to examine you while you're there, make sure it's definitely Ménière's disease that you have. You have lived with its chronicity for the last fourteen years – you are sure it's Ménière's disease that you have. He asks you to march in place with your eyes closed and arms held out, and when you do, you are dizzy and fall awkwardly to the cold, hard floor, knowing that tomorrow there will be a bruise.

Wind holds heaviness
when it speaks, so much to say.
Leaves tremble and fall.

3.

This doctor tells you to lie on the table and hang your head off of it so that
you are upside down. You would never want to be upside down. You have
Ménière's disease. When he turns your head in the direction of your bad ear
the room begins to spin, a full-blown attack, though acupuncture has kept
them at bay for the last two years. 'Stop', you say you gag you cry, 'stop.' 'This is
the treatment', he says, 'this is the treatment', the room spinning so violently
your eyes cannot keep up, nor your sanity nor stomach, and as you gag and
cry and tell him to stop he says, 'I know', though you are sure that he does
not. When finally he lets you rise you are vomiting into a dirty bin, feeling
used and small. 'You have benign paroxysmal positional vertigo', he says.
'I thought I had Ménière's', you say, desperation crowding your tiny voice;
you feel like a cartoon figure looking up with very big eyes – everything
is ridiculous and you crave kindliness. 'You do', he says, smiling as if it's a
funny joke. 'I have both?' you ask. 'You must be lucky', he laughs, and it is
like the other doctor another time, laughing when you want to talk about
your illness, which is serious. It has always been serious and unfortunately
always will be, but then this one tells you that you will be better now and you
tell him that you were fine when you came into his office. Even though the
attack exhausted you and will take days of rest to recover from, he tells you
not to lie down for forty-eight hours. You must sleep sitting up.

Broken bodies lie
when they try to tell the truth;
just like a sunset.

4.

You won't be going to the doctor again. That last one raped you, though
there were no genitals involved. He held you down and chaos reigned as the
room spun so fast your eyes couldn't keep up, nor could your stomach, and
you cry whenever you think about it. You cannot stop thinking about it and
now you are an insomniac. You have Ménière's disease and it has become
such a beast that even regular sessions of acupuncture are slow going. You
want to write a letter to the doctor to tell him he was wrong, the treatment

for benign paroxysmal positional vertigo did not work because, in fact, you have Ménière's disease. You want to ring him and tell him of the trauma of a full-blown attack, that he had no right to force you back into the darkness of your illness with its kicked-in death-prayer and here-I-am psychosis when you had entered his office a more or less healthy woman but you are warned against it by a female doctor who says he is very senior; nothing will happen. He is very arrogant and will probably laugh. She says you should only do it if talking about the incident will make you feel better. You can't feel better. You have Ménière's disease.

Screaming is easy;
just listen to birdsong at dusk
(and boulders, and wind).

Trying to Write about Ménière's Disease

1.

It was a sad day when you came to realise your body would never be glamorous holding on to the spinning Earth but did you consider it just might be closer to nature than all those other conventional bodies because it was spinning too? Why did you say 'dizzy' when the word is like 'giddy'? Is not 'falling' more appropriate to a bottom dweller with a head that follows like a little brother or sister? Tinned tomatoes, pepperoni, soy sauce, cheeses, babaganoush bought in a plastic container and the crackers that carried it to your guilty mouth: you must avoid salt though your body craves it, being so full of the ocean. You are a lost fish. Your home is an eddy. You write about sickness in bubbles plucked from underwater screams, but it cannot be an art form if the words pop before they are written. How could anyone read them?

Too many times you've wondered: if each word is monotone, why, then, should we sing? What is it to say 'poetry saves' when bile dribble stains your favourite writing dress? Or to say you're tired of back-stroking in a circle when you close your eyes to the glaring sun? Or to say when you are sleeping in your rocking bed which rides upon waves, you yourself are dreaming that you've wrapped your body in a swinging cocoon and will emerge days later, wings and all.

2.

You've forgotten silence. You never had to put it into words because you'd always known it is the Earth's phantom limb, and you, too, have felt like that: maybe more a phantom tongue than a leg while silence was a nostril inhaling everything. Now you try to place it, throwing letters like paint on a wall, writing poems all through the untameable sky: *the soundlessness of ants / or photosynthesis of plants*. You edit relentlessly, knowing 'silence' is a Big Word, like 'hatred' and 'death', so best to avoid it altogether.

Still, you want to write about the sound in your left ear. You want to say it is time's drone, molecules swimming past your head or the dam that will tug you under, but it is not natural to speak without the words you've lost amidst all the noise. None of this is natural.

3.

Once you wore a dress that fitted you perfectly. Health spilled from the top of the open neckline and below the slackened hem; your curves were so round against the silk that your body danced whenever you moved. Writing in it was like doing the rumba in your seat; sometimes ballet. Now it's like you have taken it out of the wash to find it shrunken and dripping and torn down the middle, the threads of the seams only just hanging on. When you hold it up, you see the colour has faded. As have the trees. As have the faces of your loved ones. Your favourite painting can no longer tell its story. All are shavings of dead skin filed from the memory of your earth-worn heels. Now you have a fishtail and are growing fins. You have no need of dresses because your scales would only snag the fabric. Now you are resigned to return to the place you crawled out of millions of years ago, thinking that somewhere, there must be a coral reef.

The Sick Room

Here he is, entering   though still
      a painting hung in the doorway

Once he learns to breathe again
the room is fetid and sticks in his throat

      You offer him your eyes
      which have seen new things
      and none of them have names

There is darkness between you
but outside is sunshine and *so much sex*

silverfish   earwigs   mice   going at it
     and for once
     he does not imagine going at it with you –

        you who are too weak to starve
        he who holds a bowl of soup

He offers to feed you
          spoonfuls of himself
                of heavy shoulders
     and deep silences
     after the clock chimes on the hour

        It is what he can do

He hadn't asked to get off here
              but isn't this where the bus stopped?
          Isn't this where planets aligned to form a path
       for a burning star shooting through before it disappears?

Here   he is

     and when you swallow him

by the spoonful

you are a tree growing so slowly no one can tell except the earth
you are a circle of rain before it becomes a drop

a blooming thing
a shared thing:

his very heart on your hungry tongue.

'FROM CLINIC TO CONSULTING ROOM'

FIONA WRIGHT

For as long as I've been able to recognise my illness properly, in its entirety, I've known that it is a sibling to my writing, that while they don't depend on one another, they share so much of the material that constitutes them, so many traits. This much seemed obvious: they're both an attempt to make sense of the world, to shape it, to understand or even stake out my place within it, deliberate and desperate as that may be. I don't know who I am or how to be without either of them, maybe even without them both, although I'm learning, however slowly and incompletely.

What has taken me longer to realise, I think, is that my writing can and has restored something to me that my illness so rapidly took away. When I became ill, so much of what followed, especially in the many months when the many specialists I saw struggled to find a diagnosis, was completely out of my control. My body was betraying me, and I dragged it around from clinic to consulting room, following every piece of misguided or guessworked advice that I was given, and I never once felt I had a choice. I didn't have a choice; perhaps I still don't. But writing about my illness, at times at least, has given me some control over the experiences it forced upon me, some way of navigating through them, some agency, however imperfect this may be.

Chris Kraus writes in *Aliens and Anorexia* that 'daily life turns into terror as soon as you start doubting food' and 'to question food is to question everything'[35]; when something so simple and everyday as food becomes anything but, the destabilisation is profound and terribly wide-reaching. But questioning everything is a good place for any kind of writing to begin, although I'm still not sure if this can ever be a consolation commensurate enough for what I've lost.

....

35 C. Kraus, *Aliens and Anorexia*, Los Angeles: Semiotext(e), 2000, pp. 160, 165.

Post-Treatment Care Plan

for Kahli and Nicole

We're all trying to change our spots
so it's natural we make bad puns around them.
   We're all a little bit dotty
   we always cross our t's
   out! out! damned spot!
        et cetera. The muscles stick
beneath my skin and you
have silvery scars in stripes
   along your shins and forearms.
We dance

(why walk when you can dance?)
   to the blare of beefed-up stereos
      wailing at red lights –
 it's mostly Bollywood, our fingers drill
at the fat sky

and the rain
when it comes
stabs at the asphalt:

this, it hisses, *this and this*
and this

and it smells like something new.

105

....

Her arms and legs are thin

for Pip Smith (and after T. S. Eliot)

Do I dare
Disturb the universe? Do I dare to eat a peach?
When I can't see what remains
and in short, I am afraid
and I cannot know what stands within my reach;
and there is time yet for a hundred indecisions
and a hundred visions and revisions, every time
before the taking of a toast and cup of tea.

I sit in sawdust restaurants of insidious intent
and there is time yet for a hundred indecisions. I wait.
My glass hands lift and drop a question on my plate:
do I dare to eat a steak, the squid, a peach?
Have I the strength to force the moment to its crisis?
(And they say 'But how her arms and legs are thin!')
I lick my tongue instead into the corners of the evening.

In short, I am afraid. And though I have wept and fasted
(And they say 'But how her arms and legs are thin!')
Although I've measured out my life, checked every whim,
They try to fix me in a formulated phrase
and I don't dare see what remains –
I've simply bitten off the matter with a smile.
(I know it never can be worth it, after all.)

And this is not what I meant
not it at all.

How can I spit out all the butt-ends of my days and ways,
how can I dare to eat a peach
when I know I am no prophet?
They say 'But how her arms and legs are thin!'
They say I'll learn the moment of my greatness.
They try to fix me with a formulated phrase.

They say it could have all been worth it
but this is not what I meant.

This was never what I meant.
This is not it, not it at all.

....

The numbers

have no meaning here, too
specific for everything
that they are meant to hold.

We chew each new body
up and down and over,
pick at the loose threads of jackets.
We rub
our upper arms:

five women, sometimes six,
and sometimes eight, three meals,
three snacks, three hours between,
four styles of anxious thinking, six
signs of exercise dependency.

The locum's clamlike bag
falls open at her feet:
one sandwich in blue plastic, one nectarine,
three crackers, pink wallet, keys.

There's a box of two-ply tissues on the table.
Three standard questionnaires, at twenty-eight day intervals.
I'd stopped thinking of myself
as a thing diseased.

I chew the loury fibres of a pear
that's always under-ripe, pick out
the cubes of capsicum inside the salad.

I always seem to be the only one
who cries.

There's nothing to account for any more.

'AWAY WITH THE BIRDS'

IAN C. SMITH

I overheard someone asking my partner, 'How did you first know what had happened?'

'Although he looked the same he wasn't there', she replied. 'He had gone.'

They were discussing my initial episode of transient global amnesia when I constantly repeated questions only to have both questions and answers disappear faster than youth. I now remember roughly what had occurred then, up to not long before my hospital admission, my assessment in A&E having taken some time. My next chronological memory is taking notice of the closing stages of a night cricket match on the TV above my bed. This was about four hours after admission, an unnoticed sign of my return to normality. So there is a gap of about five hours in my memory that I'll never recall now.

I have since suffered two further episodes, several years apart, which were not as bad as the first. During these I cottoned on to what was happening because of my previous experience.

'I've lost my memory again, haven't I?'

'Yes, and you've asked us this about five times now.'

My barrage of repeated questions irritates people, including family. I am aware enough to sense their intolerant or, in some instances, derisive tones of voice and body language.

Medical attention was not sought for either of these episodes, and I have managed to fight off several other near whiteouts when I struggled fiercely to remain functional. Frightening moments have come to be familiar to me as I have endured severe anxiety-induced fainting fits all of my life.

When I played rough sport I was often bruised, bandaged, sometimes in plaster. Approval was rife. It was if I wore medals of honour. But then, those wounds were nothing to do with brain, or mind, functioning. I sense what I imagine others who have medical conditions concerning the mind might feel: a kind of embarrassed fear, disapproval, or even revulsion, as if my unsteadiness, what I suffer, is shameful, or even contagious. I know it's not though because the country GP I was referred to set me straight. He looked up my condition on the Net and printed it for me.

'Let's face it, you don't get many unusual cases in general practice', he told me, stimulated. It is rare.

Of course, what helpful GPs or medical print-outs can't say is how strange it feels to hear your words and behaviour spoken of, and to have no recall of this. To some people close to me, the difference between my memory-affected self and my usual self is still a font of amusement. When I woke up in hospital after that first episode and asked the guy in the other bed where the toilet was, he told me I had been 'away with the birds' when admitted. It was obvious that I was now considered back from my airy flight, and therefore acceptable.

Transient global amnesia is a sudden temporary memory loss that can't be attributed to more common neurological conditions such as epilepsy or stroke. It is identified by its main symptom: an inability to form new memories and to recall the recent past. Commonly reported events triggering this condition include sudden immersion in cold or hot water, strenuous physical activity, sexual intercourse, medical procedures such as angiography or endoscopy, mild head trauma, and acute emotional distress, e.g. bad news, conflict or overwork. You remember who you are and recognise those you know well. Episodes are usually short-lived, and afterward your memory is usually fine. Usually but not always. Memory loss lurks, my own *bête noire*. 'We all forget things', people tell me. Yeah, I think, but some more than others.

Post-coital repercussion

Ten minutes after climax he asks if they just had sex. Although familiar with
his wisecracks, their ironic double meanings complex, she knows this is no
joke, however weird. She feels, despite him standing there, as if his essence
has disappeared. He repeats the question, unaware. When he repeats other
questions she dials, then explains what they must do, her tone matter-of-
fact, smiles, answers as if she always knew this crisis would come, masking
her worry. Then she drives, tries not to hurry.

At Admission, shamed, she sees with others his lack of inhibition, beyond
control, but he tries to please with humour, miming contrition when a nurse
says, *Drink your tea*. His ceaseless questions make them groan until a doctor
turns the key to his mind with questions of his own. Short-term memory
has wandered free. He names world leaders from years gone by. Settled in
bed, he frowns at the TV. She kisses what's left of him goodbye. They tell her
he could recover overnight. *And if not?* she thinks, her brain squeezed tight.

At midnight his prognosis remains the same. In the morning she outlines
a plan. She is still young, and not to blame. Life was never simple with this
man. She has work, children, her own friends; she calculates a fair cost
of care as she drives back in, dividends, savings, as much as she can bear.
In bed, he greets her, to her stunned surprise, that old, knowing light back
in his eyes.

....

Poet as ageing narcissist

He watches himself in the third person
at this gathering of his blood
marking a Round Figured Birthday,
hair, beard beyond mid-life grey,
not ageing well like wine or cheese,
a mockery of pulsing yesterday
which, like other damning birthday evidence,
astonishes him, and, perhaps, his clansmen.

He stands to read. They watch him
watching himself, uncertain, like him,
as he mimes patting pockets for poems,
whether to smile or exchange glances,
so they, watchers and watched,
moderate their expressions,
stay cool, will a heel-crunch of any emotion,
preferring the relief of effete jokes,
hope his voice doesn't crack like his mind.

They make him weak, they make him strong.
He knows they discuss his increasing lapses
when he drifts off to the word sanctuary,
forgetful blunders that once never were,
so makes the effort to stay in tune,
drawing close to black night's fire
though a yearning to cast off lures him
to travel light with his failing old pals,
imagination, memory, the first person.

....

Surgery

I fill my new doctor in about problems with amnesia.
She asks if I ever forget where I am when driving
so I say, Yes, but before I became an old ruin,
eating up white lines returning from holidays,
suddenly snapping from a reverie with no idea
of the previous town or the next or even what road
I travelled, foot down, elbow hot. Marvelling at this.

Sensing her duty of care to road users I suggest
surely we each experience such moments, thinking
about that drift into daydream from reality, whatever
usually occupies our minds, health, money, love,
before checking back in from grainy ticking afternoons.
Preparing my needle, she doesn't reply, perhaps
recalling a long-ago trip, the sheer *joie de vivre*.

'NAVIGATING THE SHIPWRECK COAST'

BETH SPENCER

I still find it hard to read over the poem 'The Shipwreck Coast'. Originally part of a verse memoir called *Vagabondage,* it is about such a difficult time in my life, but also an innocent one. Back when I thought the illness was just a temporary thing that would soon pass with a few months of 'rest'.

The poem also represents the first time I'd written publicly (even if obliquely) about having CFS (Chronic Fatigue Syndrome or Myalgic Encephalopathy), and a range of related conditions. So it's a kind of coming out in a way as this has been such a powerful, but to most people invisible, subtext to almost half of my life.

Vagabondage is about the year I turned fifty and sold my house and lived in a campervan. Some of its themes are the fine line between solitude and loneliness, and the idea of 'home'. These are themes that have taken on an extra edge in my life since that time after my initial diagnosis (and recalled in 'The Shipwreck Coast') when I ventured out from my shared house and friends in Sydney and had my first strange experience of the isolation that was to be repeated in smaller ways, and in ways beyond what I could have imagined, over the next twenty-five years.

Vagabondage was also my writer's rehab project. After a decade and a half of grappling with a project that was way more ambitious than my energy allowed, I could barely write for an hour without developing debilitating pain for days. Too many years of isolating myself in order to write and too many times whipping myself to the desk, despite fatigue, had led to a deep internal conflict about writing and all it meant for and in my life. So back around the time I sold my house and bought the van, I also decided to give myself permission to *not* be a writer.

Easier said than done because it was pretty much all I'd ever wanted to be, and all that was left of my ragged self-identity. (No children, partner, or defined role in the workforce, as my erratic health made all of these things a tad problematic.) Plus I had already invested so many years in the unfinished novel, and had received several grants for it (oh, the guilt).

But my body was emphatically saying *no*.

It took about seven months of using all my self-therapy tricks and tools (and I have many) before I could say, without my heart racing and without feeling sick to my stomach: '*I may never finish this novel and I don't have to be a writer*'. A relief in some ways. But it also created new challenges. During those few years it felt like something vital was lost; that an important part of me was missing.

And then, one day on the way to the supermarket (after I'd found a house again and sold the van) a thought came: what if I wrote a little book of poems about that year I lived in a campervan?

'Who reads poetry?' I thought and in this way I managed to trick myself into making it a fun project rather than a 'work' one. I also created for myself a private secret space where I could open up and be vulnerable again; a place where I could have a conversation with the world on my own terms. (Just for me.)

With poetry I could also write in fragments.

This not only suited my energy levels and erratic health, it allowed ambiguity and contradiction to have full rein (that fine line between solitude and loneliness, choice and chaos, freedom and a sense of imprisonment, the super highs and the super lows).

It also mimicked for me the fragmented nature of the self. As Maria Corti once wrote: 'A person's life does not unwind like a ball of string.' Even the supposed 'able-bodied' exist within culture as a complex of fragments; how much more so for a life where body and mind often seem deeply at odds.

And I could avoid getting stuck in the story. (A story I am always hoping will change.) I could move around inside it with more lightness and play.

With this book I set myself two aims: to make sense of that year for myself, and to learn to write with joy again. As a project it gave me both these things. Perhaps the sharpest lesson was that even when the writing is hard, I can still choose to be at ease with it. I just have to keep creating the right conditions (a small defined field, for instance, a space where I'm not at war with myself).

And it gave me much more. *Vagabondage* was published towards the end of 2014 by UWA Publishing, and the surprising feedback – the way so *many* related to its themes (the way so many people who seemed to have all that I felt I lacked could still see themselves in the story!) – was deeply moving for me, and healing in some important ways, and a coming home again.

Ten Things I Love to Hate About You

1. Someone once described it as like walking across a room in the dark and no matter which direction you go a board flies up and hits you in the face.

2. Noticing, gradually – from the subtle clues amongst the cheery posts and triumphs – the number of people in my Facebook feed who are living with a hidden illness.

3. A change of government and the social terrain shifts; suddenly feeling like a criminal again.

4. The grief for all that never was. All the books, the friendships and loves, all the children and grandchildren. All the students. All the clients. All the travels and adventures. (Scaling inner mountains instead.)

5. The exhilaration that rises with hope from a new theory or treatment or diagnostic piece of the puzzle. And then under the surface (forged by too often), bracing for the crash.

6. Writing lists of how things have improved, to remind myself. (Because it's necessary. The reminding. And it has. In a way.)

7. Writing lists of strategies and actions for the bad days when it's hard to even remember (or move) to consult such lists. But then I do. And that search for the small obscure window, pushing against and through (don't cut yourself), and then finding the next little window, and the next.

8. Salvaging a long difficult day spent prostrate by writing one not-great but not-awful poem just before midnight. (Yay.)

9. Imagining the events and parties and gatherings looked forward to with joy (but then not up to going) laid out end to end in one long glorious summer of love. A beautiful able-bodied parallel world.

10. Learning (and unlearning and learning again) to embrace the space I be. Because maybe, in the constellation of the universe, every misshapen

star, every strange permutation, is desired by life itself to be experienced and added to the mix. *The force of everything demanding everything.* Even this. Learning and unlearning, and learning it again, and again. (And again.) Until the star becomes the centre (and shines).

....

To the whales at Warrnambool

after Thomas Moore

It is said
about the dark night of the soul
that when you're in the belly of the whale
and all that you are experiencing
is blackness and stillness
and nobody knows where you are
least of all yourself
and it feels like every day there is
no change
and nothing

that the thing to know
is that the whale is always moving

your job
is simply this:

to be ready
when the time comes

and the whale
spits you out

onto a new shore.

The Shipwreck Coast

'I have seldom seen
a more fearful section of coastline'
– Matthew Flinders

Driving down the Great Ocean Road
(great ocean! great road!)
and my heart clenches.

It's twenty-one years since I drove here
in my white Toyota sedan (already a little rusty)
packed with books, files, clothes and a typewriter.

I had just been diagnosed with
chronic fatigue / post-viral blah blah whatever
and I needed rest I was told.

Fresh air seemed a good idea too.

Sydney – way too crazy busy.
And here was this house,
vacant most of the winter,
cheap enough – and across the road – the ocean!

(A little sea-bathing to set me up forever.)

I had to learn to drive again
after a decade of buses, trains and walking.
A little skittery at first.

And I had to dismantle my life.

But hey, it was already crumbling.

While I'd just ended a long deep relationship,
my friends were busy nesting –
moving in with partners, buying houses,

consolidating careers, creating babies.

So goodbye job, goodbye share house,
farewell most of my possessions.

*

(Now) at the end of a gravel road
in the national park
I stop my Van, make a cup of tea
and watch the remaining Apostles
lovingly, savagely
being eroded by the waves.

Two millimetres a year, say the guidebooks,
with now and then a larger block calving
into the ocean, like the way London Bridge
fell apart in the middle.

Peterborough, the tiny town (one-shop-one-hotel)
where I stayed all those years ago
– at the start of my crazy shipwrecked
twenty-one years –
is next along.

*

I feel an enormous
sadness

for that thirty year old
who thought 'rest'
meant going off alone, with a typewriter
and a few reams of paper.

(Feeling weak and vulnerable?
Try something harsh and challenging,
That'll do it.)

*

Back then, within a month of arriving
I was diagnosed with more acronyms.

And so began even more
renunciation, relinquishing, peeling away.

No more wheat-rye-barley-oats-dairy-pork-
lamb-potatoes-tomatoes-lettuce-chillies-
spices-eggplants-capsicum-egg whites-
cucumber-citrus-bananas-tap-water…
And of course no alcohol or caffeine.

(I was so shocked and so hungry
when I got the results,
that I ate a meat pie!
Last meal of the condemned.)

But I was exhausted
and broken open,
willing to try anything.

I bought soy milk, rice flour and dried beans
and made lots of soups and stews,
flavouring them with goats milk yoghurt
(which as one friend said, tasted a little
like a goat's armpit).

But look! The ocean!
Who could ever be unhappy with the ocean
just across the road? And books, and paper?

(It's going to be great! – the *great* ocean –
I'll finish my book,
I'll get well again…)

*

It was the tail end of winter when I arrived
and for weeks everything was
grey and beige.

Grey sky. Grey ocean. Greyish sand.
The grey-green rock stacks in the Bay of Martyrs.
And the vast constantly moving
grey of the wind-pruned scrub that stretched
inland and west as far as I could see.

The house – last on a street
of mostly holiday houses
vacant at this time of the year –
was disappointingly drab.

Hardi-plank. Not a stitch of plant life
except for the wind-mown couch.

Beige carpet, beige walls,
olive-green laminex,
fake woodgrain cupboards.

There was a deck but it was too exposed
to the wind and the rain to ever sit out there.

*

I learnt to set a good fire.

My ritual (on a good day)
was to come in from my 'office'
(a bedroom off the deck)
just as the sun began to roll down and
wash the sky a darker grey.

I'd light the fire, turn on the television

(which only got one channel)
and watch *Degrassi Junior High*.

(I dreamt about the characters at night.)

       *

Outside, the plastic drink bottles full of water
that were strategically placed around
a neighbour's yard beguiled me into thinking
that I'd landed in an
awful, empty but prim suburbia.

Until one morning I woke to find that dogs
had torn apart a rabbit on my front lawn.

My last residence had been Bondi.
Blue sky, blue-green ocean, yellow sand.
Life, food, colours, rich textures, rich smells and
sounds…

The grey beige relentlessness of my haven,
and the constant howling ripping of the wind
ate into my brain.

And then just as I was about to crack
one morning the sun came out.

And the wind relented just a little.

And I fell instantly in love.

       *

I wrote letters.
(No phone, and long before the
days of mobiles or email.)

If I could manage, I would sit for a while
at my makeshift desk
and look out over the crazy
wild horses in the ocean and the majestic Martyrs
– those rock islands rising squat and solid
out of the water, crowned with
wind-harried but tenacious green,
and circled by birds.

Every day that I could,
I walked on the beach.

I loved the drift-woody feel under my hand
of the staircase leading down from the
top of the cliffs.

Sometimes the bottom steps
were buried under sand dumped overnight
by the waves. Every day
a little different.

When the sun glinted on the cliffs,
revealing a jewel box of colours
and layers of lines and textures,
it was like walking amid prehistoric towers.

*

I stopped wearing make-up and dying my hair
– for the chemicals, but also
because the birds and the wind didn't care.

I wore the same baggy clothes
day after day.

I became salty and weathered
and rarely bothered to look
into the tiny mirror in the laundry

unless it was shopping day in Warrnambool
or a rare trip to Melbourne to see friends.

*

I became slightly reckless as a driver.
I loved the trip each week to do the shopping,
and even the journey to Melbourne,
though it exhausted me for days afterwards.
But it filled me with joy when I
rounded the bend on the home stretch
and saw the sheep in the soft lumpy paddocks
and beyond them the ocean.
I'd sing to myself and yell out
to the sheep and the waves, as loud as I could.

Until one day three little birds on the road
failed to get out of the way,
and I heard them – boop boop boop –
and saw them fly up a short way in the air
through my back window
and crash down onto the asphalt.
I slammed on the brakes, but it was done,
and I drove slower after that.

*

– Being back meant
lighting the fire,
putting on a cup of green tea,
and *Degrassi*… (those sweet passionate
young things, so hard not to worry about them
while I was away).

*

At night, before bed, I put the fire out with the
teapot and I learnt to move the big armchair

up against the front door
so it wouldn't blow open.

Some nights I would lie under my borrowed
doonas and blankets with the wind screaming,
the windows rattling and the walls shaking.
And when I'd finally
fall asleep I'd wake suddenly from dreams
of waves crashing in through the glass doors
a few feet from my bed.

*

I paddled through the days,
and then a letter would come –
a rejection or an opportunity lost –
and I would sink.

(Shattered.)

I'd rise eventually, of course.
Buoy myself up.
And then something else,
(something so small)
and I would come to grief again.

*

Rising and sinking.
Is that a form of swimming?

*

As the months passed and I didn't 'recover'
– and as the pages didn't fill up
(somehow my brain just didn't work like it used to)
a steady numbness set in. A deep shock.

*

Meanwhile, the bouts of exhaustion were like
nothing I'd ever experienced.
Deep and bone-stripping.
Frightening in their intensity.

Some days it felt like my chest
had been carved out with a knife and there was
nothing, no life force.

Most days my head felt like
a bucket of shit filled with razor blades.

Perhaps the worst was being so exhausted
and yet too wired to sleep.
Every nerve painfully alert.

*

The feelings could be so total
it was hard to remember what it felt like
to not be overwhelmed by the slightest task.

Hard to believe that this mysterious thing
energy – that connects us
to ourselves, and to each other –
could ever be mine to command again.

And then bewilderingly it would pass.

And then it would come back again.

*

Rising and sinking.

I've learnt to live better with it, although it

can still capture me so fully that it is
terrifying.

But struggling and panic only make it worse.

Patience. Let the waves
take you for a bit.

(But what to do with the
anger, when you can barely *breathe*
let alone move
to get it out of your body?)

*

Back then, on the days when I felt good
I loved the solitude
and the wildness.

As the weather warmed a little
I would look out my window and see people walking
on my beach.
(*My* beach! How dare they?)

I would gather driftwood
to add to the fire
and barely wonder where it came from,
how it turned up in my world.

Although once I found
a dead penguin on the beach,
its feathers slicked with oil.

Everything, after all, just a step away.

*

At the end of the five months

my tenancy was up, the house
wanted by holiday-makers,
and I had to make my way back to the city.

My car a little rustier.
My bank balance dipping
further into the red.

*

One afternoon in that last week, a blue wren came
and perched on the driver's side mirror
while I was backing out the car.

It chatted to me and to its reflection for ages.

And I cried when it left, because
I wanted so badly to believe
it had a message for me.

*

I reach the Bay of Martyrs
just as the sun is setting
and pull the Van in amongst a forest of buses.

Across the road, the house, still there.

Beaten by the wind,
perhaps a little greyer,
strangely unchanged.

I watch it for a long time.
Then I turn and look out to the ocean
and consider following the wooden steps
down to the beach.

(My beach.

All that beauty,
all that rage.)

But the light is leaving quickly
and the sand is cold.

People are filing into their buses
and the doors clanging shut.

I close my eyes and listen to the waves,

then continue on.

'OF JAWS AND JIGSAWS'

MARGARET OWEN RUCKERT

What informs my writing? Let me sort through my jigsaw of a past to join up the dots and mix metaphors for a more inclusive result. Working from the corners of the puzzle will frame my endeavours. First: observations. Does pain inform anything more than an absence of harmony? And how apt that dislocation inversely implies the preferred state of being.

One early puzzle piece is sky-blue with clouds of uncertainty. I have always been interested in health, even though it was often not interested in me. As a child of six years, I contracted whooping cough, undiagnosed for quite a while. But my recovery period is remembered only by activity, albeit a sedentary one. I would paint large white lilies, cut from their clump near the garden tap. Could whooping cough's legacy explain my sad swimming endeavours? Never made twenty metres at high school.

There must be gems of information from childhood hidden away in our memory vaults which, if opened, would reveal strange treasures. Our *whys* and *why nots* – our life puzzles – might find answers. The *why* of writing is often answered with *why not*, simply because there is no because.

Closer to now, my memory pieces retain more substance. A dislocated jaw made itself a monster when I was psyching up to return to teaching full-time with two young children. I never knew the entire story: teeth-grinding in my sleep, jaws sliding on tough carrot, a rubble of genes? After a splint was made to alleviate pain, the jaw slowly returned to its home ground. But it was a restless jaw and over the next thirty years, I was to be reminded of the symptoms of temporomandibular joint pain (TMJ), and still am.

Teaching and TMJ were never friends. In the months following the dislocation, I wore the splint to work. Its removal was fraught, as the jaw, like an explorer, could wander far from home. After some time – I've no idea how long – the splint was mainly worn at night. Of course, jaws and teeth are connected as a jigsaw. After dental work I remember lying on the floor, as though knocked out. Painkillers were no match for this condition, a puzzle in itself.

But the life pieces I am discovering come from the sort of box found in holiday houses, a mix of many puzzles that with time and patience can be worked out. The mystery for me in undertaking this essay was basically: why did I start writing? I checked diaries. The year after the dislocation saw my first published article on teaching. More articles followed, together with a column in the college newsletter.

At this time I began writing fiction and poetry. But, being a science teacher and lacking tertiary studies in the arts, I was wary of sending my work out. An opportunity to take creative writing in my master's degree led to a distinction and spurred me on. My two books of poetry, *You Deserve Dessert* and *musefood,* both feature, as you might expect, foods, especially soft and comfort foods. The experience of a colonoscopy to investigate anaemia (TMJ > chewing steak is painful > chocolate shakes are beautiful > little iron in diet) resulted in the poem 'Parched'.

And now? Dental work is still a killer category for me, the piece of my life jigsaw that remains out of place. I ask for more time, hold my jaw and wait for the aftershocks. TMJ? What's that? Oh!

parched

before the operation, instructions said:
    no water under the sun
my body limp, limper, whimpering
internal surface like forgotten earth
waterless, parched as lava pavement
raving, volcano shaking
earthquake nerved and dehydrating
I call the doctor

'nothing by the mouth, nothing wet
before general anaesthetic'

no suck of ice, no sip of normalcy
don't they test their own medicine

nervous system lasers flash
hot/cold advice/advice
electrolyte imbalance is
fractured body
language in 1000
different tongues

I am the sum total of Babel
falling as a brittle insect wing
to break on dirt
did I say 'hurt?'

life is aquatic on a saline drip
please keep up your liquids
dehydration is
delirium

devil's work

....

house of panic

bathroom
one unhinged mirror
one angry jawline
frozen mid-sentence

kitchen
anger in bite-sized portions
if teeth slip on raw carrot
diagnose anxiety, blame a vegetable

hall
a hideous wall of angry portraits
all with susceptible chins
and no escape at the vanishing point

lounge room
leisure in negative space
angry scenes, knowing nothing can help you
and this was a quiet neighbourhood

study
night refuge of the angry
cushions in space, soft landing
on a higher rage

veranda
den of alternative respite
take the anger bomb outside
to tick away in the fresh air of peace

family room
famed for its angry laughter
hear familiar jokes about your body
explain it wasn't all your fault

bedroom
anger of sleep proportions
body reliving the past 24 pains
wall-to-wall nightmare

strong surgery

a non-delicate smell leaks from the aisle seat in front of me, sitting there is a body with greying wisps of hair, in fact, mostly bald, must be due for the other side by now, why am I so cruel, life's a one-way road out of here, no sign of a bypass, she's reading today's obituaries, why tempt fate, she must really want to be taken, wearing that eye shadow for the final photo, neon blue competing with the rest of her face, tormented leather, closest match would be an elephant's leg, remembering my childhood visits to the zoo, as for her neck, the slump of a bunya tree at its base, holds up her soul, but now the evidence stings me, a neuron fire, she must be the smell in the carriage, I look again, surreptitiously

she's a mass of lumps, concealed by a bright red gel, but why would a health company make a point of pain, why the colour red, surely out of compassion, dye the treatment a skin tone, I look away in case she's suspicious, perhaps she already is, producing a sun-yellow beanie, thank goodness no pompom, and pulling it securely down over the lumps, everything is out of sight now, I'll be one of the few to put a face to the smell, though the cap looks suspicious, no one could ignore this bright knitted cap on a spring day, covering a definite hole in the back of her head, I saw right through it of course

she's just had day surgery, don't we all eventually, when you leave you feel more wounded than on admission, she's journeying home to heal, sunshine yellow probably matches her kitchen curtains or perhaps gazanias, daffodils, yes she looks like she might have had the strength once to deal with a cancerous garden, now she's a public specimen, a living set of symptoms of a failing health system, at least send her home in a taxi, nurse, or else she'll catch something unpronounceable, one more statistic, one less statistic where it counts, the hospital waiting lists, she's already starting to sneeze, innocent woman watches as monster germs invade and overtake a fellow traveller, I hope they did the right cut on the right person, could this woman be a premonition to me, a glimpse of my future, after years of semi-starvation, bird bones, RSI, TMJ, I could go on, not to expect too much, just another drug trial, I'll be an early adopter, a gracious volunteer, make a train trip the high of my day, and a yellow-striped beanie to scare away the lows

'FRAGMENT: THE BODY WRITING IN EXCESS'

QUINN EADES

How do we write the body? How do we write the sick body, the broken body, the different and differing body, the screaming body, the body in pain, the dying body, the falling/flying body? How do we take *matter* and place it into language without entering an echo chamber of representation? What does it take to spread cells on a page, to open up cavities and veins? And when I ask how do *we*, I am also asking how do *I*. I am asking what becomes possible when I write this body, that 'is always moving towards the fragment, towards disintegration, towards a quantum state of here and not-here'.[36]

In his exquisite essay 'Corpus', philosopher Jean-Luc Nancy suggests that the word 'body' could in fact be a stand-in for the words 'in excess', and points to the impossibility of pinning any body to a page. In the very next sentence, he writes that this *in excess* is actually nothing (and that by inference, the body is also nothing); that '*body* does not exceed language by anything, being a word like any other'. That this body, which is a word like any other, carries the 'always possible imminence of a fracture and of a spontaneous outpouring of the *word* itself...*Body*, like a piece of bone, a pebble, a stone, a granule, falls right where we need it' (author's italics).[37]

If *body* falls right where we need it, then it falls here, in writing, in the fragment, in poetry. If *body* is (and is not) *in excess*, then the sick and chronically ill body is excess itself. It is excretion, excrement, excoriation: it is ex (or X). *Body* (X) marks the spot, it is away from and out; it is too much. It oozes and leaks, is unstable and unpredictable, it falls or stutters, it fails measurements and doesn't hit percentiles – on the hospital forms there are all those boxes that will be crossed with this X to describe in a strange kind of code what is wrong. And this code, this X that crosses boxes, that is the ex in excess, is the body in writing, is the body pushing

....

36 Q. Eades, *all the beginnings: a queer autobiography of the body*, North Melbourne: Tantanoola, 2015.

37 J.-L. Nancy, *Corpus* (R. A. Rand, Trans.), New York: Fordham University Press, 2008.

out from and into language, is the body announcing itself, again and again and again.

I could tell you now all of the ways in which this body that writes these words is sick. You may guess some of that sickness from the poems that come next, or you will want me to tell you, to make my own corpus of what is not 'well'. There is always the urge to know, to ask 'but what *is* it that's wrong?'

What is wrong

Back: at thirteen I bent over to put on a pair of shorts in a speedboat and bulged a disc in my lower back. I spent two weeks in a bottom caravan bunk on codeine and one night woke up floating, my head banging into the bunk above me. Now, once or twice a year, I bend over innocuously, and my back goes into spasm and I am locked.

Muscles and nerves: I've been told I'm hyper-flexible, but that this is not a good thing. I'm prone to overuse injuries. At twenty-five I injured my right elbow, shoulder, and neck, and was told I'd never work again. Various muscle and nerve diagnoses have been posited but never pinned down. I live with chronic pain down my right side, which I mostly choose to ignore.

Brain chemistry: the first time there were concerns about depression and anxiety I was nine. My mother would come in and find me staring up at the ceiling, wide awake. 'Sweetheart, what is it?', she'd ask and I would list worries for her, and pick my fingernails until they bled, and not sleep. By twenty-one I was on antidepressants and have spent more time on medication than off.

Lungs: asthma, first diagnosed at seventeen, disappeared in my early adulthood, but has now taken up a firm residence in my chest. Steroids most winters, preventers every day, triggers that range from dust to pungent smells in supermarket cleaning aisles, and never going anywhere without a puffer and spacer.

Ovaries: polycystic ovarian syndrome (PCOS), and all that this disease brings (periods of infertility, increased risk of endometrial cancer, diabetes and heart disease, emergency surgeries to remove one ovary and tether the other to my pelvic wall).

Thyroid: Hashimoto's thyroiditis. An autoimmune disease in which the body eats the thyroid. Daily medication, regular blood tests to check thyroid-stimulating hormone (TSH) levels. The easiest of the lot in some ways, except that it wasn't diagnosed until my mid-twenties, and a low-functioning thyroid can be a contributing factor in severe and untreatable depression, and when I think of the gland in my neck being eaten away I remember those five years when I almost never went outside, or made eye contact, or wrote. I remember being on an antipsychotic that was so strong I had to take it lying down. I remember knowing I would never be well.

So yes, I have given you a corpus of sorts, but now I say this: the sick body is the strong body, the fighting body, the body brave enough to disorganise, to be in excess. The sick body is the body that knows it is dying, and turns towards that moment, and insists on being seen.

Reverberation

They X-ray my lungs as if looking through
me will tell them something: as if
those graining grey pictures will help.

Do you have any metal on? Yes. I
have nipple rings, I say. There is
always silence when I say this. Always because
my lungs have been looked at more than
once. Because when I go to hospital they like to press me
against a lined plate, shivering, breath held, to hunt down
shadows and crushed glass; to capture the crackle and wheeze.

They know these rings are not for them.

Silver looping through flesh, a gasping shout.

In hospitals, steel and desire do not mix.
In hospitals, steel is for cannulas and speculums, for cracking
chests, for the legs of whining beds.

Yes, I have nipple rings, I say. And there it is: the absence
of noise that is not silence, that comes after speaking, out
of place.

It is what is left after the shot has rung out
it is everything drilled down to quiet in the aftermath
it is the tinnitus ring, the screaming din. It is the sound
of death, reverberating.

The X-ray is done. Shiver and breathe. Later mist, and blood
pressure cuff, and the way hospital gowns unwrap me, the way they conspire
to show more than they cover. The obscene white and blue. The incessant
beeping. The groans from the next bed, because there are always groans
from the next bed.

In between, nothing.

The early morning hours roll out from under me.

Water gathers, unheard, underneath my silver-plated ring.

When I take it off the next day it has left a red and blistered band around
my right index finger.

I have been scalded by love, by jewellery, by the meeting point of trapped
fluid, and skin.

Two days later, on the train, I notice the blister
has dried and I can't help but pick at it. Peel it. Pull it away.

Coruscating, the skin flakes fall to the glittering ground. The people
around me
tap at their phones and carefully pretend my cells are not travelling, drily,
to meet them.

Coalesce

~~I am already dead.~~ Already, I am dead.
~~I am gone.~~ Already, I am gone.
   You are reading this when I am gone.

Dis. Integrate.

Already I am earth   ash   leaf   caterpillar,
the tomato between your teeth.

Already I am ink on the page the bottom
of your boot tepid water from a sun
soaked tap, wood.

Dis. Integrate.

Already I am dust mote that cannot fit
inside itself, small parts flung out and
around and under, blood shiver, glass shard,
prism throwing light at the yellow kitchen walls.

Already I am dug down with a sign skewered
above me in the soft dirt my children dug out
earlier: this is the grave where I lay, where
I lie, where I am folded inside a pillow case.
I am my own terrier tucked in, dead from
the green syringe the vet brought to our house
at eleven am. My arm shaved.
Anaesthetic put in. I am the dream of dirt
and bone. I am put down. I am put under.
I am touching root systems, gravel, earthworm.

I am carried by me and my three year old
who cradles my head while I take
the weight of my body.
My eyes refuse to close.
My tongue keeps pushing out

between the loose points of my teeth.

Dis. Integrate.

~~I am gone.~~ Already, I am gone.

Absorption

My outsides gather rain
from the air. I cycle through.
My outsides gather wetness as I pass.
My outsides draw water through
the barrier of my skin because it is not
a barrier. Because it is full
of holes. Because this is the very definition
of porousness. My outsides
gather rain from the air.

The layer underneath my skin
is desperate for the wetness of the day.
Dry too long, it wants a damp
salvation.

How are you dry? They ask this, when I pass.
You are all fat and blood and tissue.
You are already mostly water.

They will never know all
of the ways I am dried and desiccated;
how paper lives underneath my skin;
how bark has taken the place of organs;
how rough the core of my abdomen is;
how there is sandpaper between my thighs;
that my heart is a balloon filled with sand.

When it squeezes, it bulges
like a soft ball held too hard.
It protrudes top and bottom; you can see
the outlines of grit.

My outsides are desperate
to drink the day. Absorption
is the method. Wetness
the outcome, but like desire

it will be fleeting and unsatisfied
and after the peddles have stopped peddling,
and I am
        inside
out of the rain, I will always
be dry again. The sand will win. I will be
a bag of grain. I will seek damp. I will try
to lick it from the insides of your cheeks the next time we meet.

You will not understand, and find me too needy. We
will turn from each other. One dry, one wet. Nothing damp. No leaks.

'MY OWN OTHER SELF'

KRISTEN LANG

When I meet people who begin to become important to me, there generally comes a time when not telling them about my childhood mental illness starts to feel like a deception. Why is that? The illness started, more or less, when I was eleven, with a slow slide into what from the outside, where it was noticed at all, must have seemed like a sad and perverse obsession. On my thirteenth birthday I was hospitalised. By then the odd decisions my brain was making were causing me to become physically ill. I didn't feel unwell at the time. I felt secretive – I was doing things I couldn't tell people about. But I also felt, in a strange, half-strangled way, euphoric. I was worryingly underweight, having been slowly starving myself for almost two years. I still don't know why. It wasn't about body image. Certainly, I wanted to be noticed. More than that, I wanted to be a genius. And I wanted to be loved. But then I was loved and I was being noticed. And while it's a fair guess that there were some anxieties about the genius part, the pain I now associate with the experience really only surfaced in the humiliation that began with my treatment. Part of the problem was the question of how to acknowledge the 'stupidity', which is to say the sickness, that was my behaviour. Anorexia is a compulsion – I knew what I was doing and yet at the same time a larger part of my thoughts didn't care whether I knew or not, being too busy with bigger things (eating less, exercising more). Breaking out of this compulsion left a shuddering hole in my sense of direction, not to mention my sense of self and my sense of pride.

To an extent, I guess it's obvious that the freefall phase of my anorexic life was always going to land badly. Still, the degree of difference between that time and the time of getting well again disturbs me even now. My two months in hospital and the years that followed seem to have gouged themselves into my psyche, largely because of the nature of the illness, but partly too because of the medical response that was provided. The treatment I received could easily have been better.

On my thirteenth birthday, I was placed in an isolation ward (a single room) and was not allowed to leave unless I was in a wheelchair someone else was pushing. It wasn't that I couldn't walk. In truth, I could run and had been awarded school girls' sports champion a few months earlier. I was instructed to use bedpans for toileting, my bins were checked, and the sink in the room was blocked. I was not the most extreme of anorexics, I had never been bulimic, and none of my organs were failing, so I guess this must simply have been the standard response. A kind of mental shock treatment designed to convince me that all was not well.

What shook me most was a specific list of personality traits one of my psychiatrists presented to me – I remember his smile as he explained to me that these were the traits officially associated with my disease. I ticked almost all of them. I *was* this disease. And I had to wonder if there was anything in me that *wasn't* this disease. It was a loss-of-identity moment that would haunt me for the next decade. And beyond. I had bad dreams about my psychiatrists for quite a while and still have an immediate dislike of people in plain-coloured turtleneck skivvies, which is very unfair of me. I don't think this dislike was born only of the fact that they were the ones taking away my power, robbing me of my euphoria, guiding me back to a perspective that wasn't going to kill me. I think it was also that they evidenced for me the lie in that old adage 'what doesn't kill you makes you stronger'. In their attempts to treat the disease I think they failed to consider the treatment itself as an experience that might leave a less than useful mark. It's hard to tell of course. I had a mental instability. Perhaps I was always going to carry a sense of dysfunctionality, regardless of the methods of rescue. I hope that's not always the case.

I did also meet some more than beautiful people as a result of my illness – several exceptional nurses, and, as I was slowly given more freedom to move around, some truly wonderful sick people (other patients), of which, in this world, there are many. In other ways, too, the experience was a learning curve, impacting on my sense of what matters, and on my sense of what brains are and how we live with and through them. Was it a chronic illness? Undoubtedly yes. Another delightful insight offered to me by the same psychiatrist was this: what was wrong with me, he said, while it might ebb in its current form, would very likely reappear in other forms throughout my life. Again, not a useful conviction to plant in the anxieties of a thirteen year old – did he think I deserved fair warning? Who knows. In any case, anorexia is rarely a thing that leaves quickly. I skirted its edges, unable to let go, not knowing what else to hang on to, for years. In my first year at university, somewhat predictably, I dipped back into it a little more deeply for a number of months and ended up dropping out of my course and into depression.

Chronic illness will always impact on a person's sense of self – it's not the same as catching the flu. This is as true, I think, for mental illnesses as for other kinds of pain. One becomes dysfunctional on possibly multiple levels and the challenge of responding strongly in areas that might combat that dysfunctionality is not always easy to face. There's an element of grief in finding oneself wrenched miles from the person one might otherwise have been, the person one thought one was, the dreams once entertained. Many of us have that experience, of course, with or without chronic illness.

I do not know how my life would have been different without the experiences I've had. I am part of a study now that suggests there are genetic contributions or susceptibilities. Other research points to a relationship with gut flora. Really, it doesn't matter. I am what I am. And I suspect I do not feel so different in my joys and struggles from so many others. Most of us have moments in our lives that are disturbing for years at a time, if not decades. Most of us carry flaws. Most of us are also, in some ways, and on certain days, beautiful.

So why is it I feel the need to present my childhood illness to those I am getting to know? And to all of you who read this now as well? I told my history to the man who is now my husband after the first time we made love. Was it a confession? A warning? Mostly I think I am trying to find a way around the elephant in my mind. And perhaps I have managed to do that only in the last decade or so. The last person I told gave me a memory of his own as a kind of exchange. His memory was of a forsythia bush in bloom outside his granny's home. It was the kindest thing I think anyone has ever given me. Now, when I think of my illness, it is coloured yellow. And the world is a better place. People are amazing. And this, I guess, is what it all comes down to in the end. Whatever our illness, whatever our pain, and whether or not our particular pain would make it into an anthology such as this one, we remain creatures able to give and receive kindnesses, creatures capable of love, creatures capable of responding to our own next moment. For all these things, may we always find optimism.

....

Hole

The dark breaks on the sea of its own rising,
a moonless tide swelling into shadow. At its centre,
a woman stands on a float of leaves, on their reds
and browns, their veins decaying and the not-

night waiting below. The black leans into her blood, full
and heavy with emptiness. Balancing on the leaves'
frail bones, she barely moves. In her heart, a stuttered
cry:...*this...this way...this way now*. But the dark

swirls and the sound is swallowed. Her eyes
dig for the fall. She is held by a wire, the thin
clamour of her pulse.

....
Luthier

There is a wooden post inside the cello –
the luthier is tinkering. If it slips, the body cannot hum
and the strings, thin and strange, hold only the shadow
of a melody. I tell him the ribs have tightened. I touch
the sternum – here, I say. He taps the chest – sing, he says,
fingers nudging the heart.

....

The small house of her body

(i)
In the small house of her body,
under the flooring, the crossbeams
have buckled. She can feel how the walls

lean, the floorboards
nudging under rugs and tables.
Yet all her doors still open. The sun

still fills her windows. And the days
roll on without war or plague –
she is clothed, there is food on the table.

When she speaks, another voice
mumbles through the shadows of her body,
an under-self, seamless,

like a pact she has signed
in secret, not by choice. She is the nest
some cuckoo has taken, the chick

already hatched, wet still and calling, calling
under the house. A thin, chest sound,
as if the bird's beak will not open.

(ii)
To feed the bird, she cuts
into her bones with the steel edge
of her hunger, mixing the dust

with her blood and soaking it
into the bird's closed mouth.
She barely eats, standing guard

at the slow powdering of her hips
and of her spine, her flesh vanishing.

She is light, and the crossbeams loosen, her feet

scarcely tie her to the ground. She sweeps
a distant gaze through the skyline
of herself – a faint mirage. The bird

calls and the raw heat of her blind,
befuddled heart thins
in the blue arcs of her fingers.

She runs. For months. A year. The transport
of her drug inks into all of her body. She is
shrewd. Slips under those she loves

in the riptide of compulsion. And yes,
she knows. And no, she will not choose
to break away. Her paths tilt and the days

are like falling – each step trickles
into the same dim room. The past
echoes in the hung

hollows of her skin…She is need,
viral in her body's cells, her bones
a strange memento.

(iii)
She does not die. In the children's ward,
two brothers drown slowly
in the effusions of their lungs.

A young girl spasms with a disease
of the old. Another has the skin of her legs
stretched across her arms to heal the burns

that went so close to taking all of her.
The thin girl is kept apart and as idle
as shelving, inert under the weight of being well.

She would run, even now, from the slow pull
of gravity. But is held. Her room wraps
around her. And printed on the walls –

how the world, saving her, will find her faceless
and carry on. Did she need saving? She cannot
see herself in mirrors. The cuckoo is large.

She stays, bedpans
and trays of tepid food beside her.
And she is watched. And each week

she is weighed on the antique scales
in the corridor. She eats. And cradles
in her hands, like a held breath, the gap

between the disease scrawled on her chart
and the torn haze of what she has done, herself
in the phrases she has become.

She looks at her fingers as she feeds.
At the house of herself – how the floor
wavers at her feet. And at the satin-eyed

psychiatrists, like ravens on the ruins, their words
draped over joists and lintels. She has
no light for the shadows she has made,

no torch for the nest inside her, the bird
still burrowing. And the medics of her mind
address a child she doesn't know, moons

from where she lives. She cries at one of them. Sinks
into his chest. Like a foreign coin in his hands. Smells
only the illness. And this, she thinks,

is the insanity, this touch, meaning nothing, her name
printed at her wrist and none of it real.

She is scared. The ground blurs and she cannot

move but to fumble, her brain-worm inside her,
its twists woven with her will. She blinks.
Her brown eyes dissolve behind their lids, each

iris lifts under patchwork wings. And not
all of her can return. Two wasps fly
from her pools of eyes. And in her palms,

the fold-lines stain to show the corrosion.
In the small house of her body, books
lie scattered. There are pages, half-pages

missing under the floor. She hovers
in the story of herself. Sells it to the day,
and in the night – the echo

of the lines that are absent. She is
heavier. Inside and out. Discharged,
she knows she is vulnerable.

(iv)
The years are made of breath
and slow confusions. She is more honest –
light through the perforations of the self.

She finds there is no junction
marked to show she is well again.
No rebirth of the mind, no chrysalis to unfold.

Days slide into days. And she loves,
in the gaps that remain, how the wind
and the stars blow through her.

How the day-night floats its wide expanse
through her rooms, sky seeping through the underfloor
dark, and the thin birds almost flying.

'MULTIPLE SHEEP'

DAVID BROOKS

I have MS, an ironic disease for a writer. The same initials signify 'manuscript'. I smile when publishers or other writers ask me how my MS is going. My MS affects principally my right arm and leg (more jokes there…). I had it for thirty years without knowing. There are different kinds of MS. I think I'd prefer mine to all but one of the others, as it's not relapsing/remitting, which is to say it does not come in numerous debilitating episodes, each one leaving one more permanently devastated. Mine is Secondary Progressive, which manifests at first with a fairly major illness that one recovers from, though it leaves residual damage – scars (sclerae) on the brain and/or spinal cord – then resurfaces. It might not surface again for many years, when new lesions appear on the brain or spinal cord and there's a bit more residual damage, perhaps of a different kind.

My first episode was when I was twenty-five. For a short while, I was paralysed from the waist down. I was diagnosed as having had a transverse myelitis, roughly a brief viral ringbarking of the spinal cord. If it came back within seven years, I was told, then it was probably MS. MS was difficult to diagnose. They didn't have MRIs at that time. The paralysis never recurred, though gradually, over the years, I developed what I call my bad leg. I assumed I had Guillain-Barré syndrome, since there'd been an epidemic of this while I was in North America, touched off by vaccinations for swine flu, and I'd had such a vaccination. Then six or seven years ago, thirty years after my paralysis, my right hand started to go. I began to doubt the Guillain-Barré theory and thought I'd better see a neurologist. Within minutes of the MRI I was told I had MS. The MRI revealed no new lesions and suggested that all my lesions and all my damage were rather ancient. Recently, however, I had a second full MRI and found I now have new lesions. It seems the kraken is stirring.

A year after the MS diagnosis (2010) I had a 'silent' and painless heart attack – touchy coronary arteries are in my genes – and now have three stents, so I guess my chronic condition is twofold. What to say? I've always worked on the principle of use-it-or-lose-it and try to keep as fit as I can (swimming, exercise bike); I'm not in a wheelchair yet – I hope that's at least a decade off – but do walk, haphazardly, with a crutch. The crutch – apparently this is common and predictable – has brought on carpal tunnel syndrome in my 'good' hand. Most recently the general wear and tear on the body from so much lopsidedness has also brought on some initial osteoarthritis. I joke about the seven plagues.

Yet, paradoxically, my life has never been so good. I've left academia, which had held me a fairly willing captive for thirty-five years, and haven't missed it for a moment. I can write full-time when I want to and when I have something I need to write, and I find that this is almost all the time. I live on what one might (generously) describe as a little farm, high in the mountains in New South Wales, with a few sheep rescued from industrial farming. Occasionally I see joy in them, and the joy that this brings me is almost indescribable. My wife and I have been vegans for just over a decade. It's not *cured* me in any obvious way but I wonder how much worse I'd be, physically, if I *weren't* so, and it's not, in any case, for our health, it's for the animals.

Clearly my disabilities are there, every second of the day, in every step I take, every attempt I make to carry something, but overall I don't give much *weight* to them. You learn to work around them, become inventive. A great many things can still be done if they're done slowly, and there can be worse scars on the brain than the physical. In a way my woundedness has been a kind of healing, or contributed to it. It's helped open my eyes. A very different kind of life begins when one gets over oneself. Any suffering, incapacity or curtailment I've experienced or am likely to experience is nothing compared to the suffering of animals and the distortion and curtailment of their lives through human intrusion and intervention. As a writer I know why I am here and what I have to do – an astonishing gift, when you think about it – and that is to write and fight for them, and intrude as little as possible.

Cleaning the Gutters

Each day is like a brimming glass.
You have to carry it so carefully.
This morning Danny turned up
to clean the gutters and re-
point a portion of the roof and
from the ladder I can no longer climb
told me about his childhood in Donegal
dropping on the worn
paths that the sheep have made
the black, mulched leaves
for me to pick up later, use
to line the pots I've set aside
for the tomato and basil plants. It was to be
my writing time but no
matter: the sheep
were so curious to see
a human walking on the roof and I
still find a disc of warm spring sun
glistening between my fingers.

Spiders about the House

Up here in the mountains it's funnel-web country,
build a house and it draws them around,
every basement a Chartres or a Coventry,
every low window a trawling-ground:
garden with gloves on, take care
when you're under the deck,
touch a trip-wire and you summon them,
move a log too quickly
and one might leap at your neck.
They come up through the floorboards
to escape the wet, roam widely in springtime
looking for a mate, can get aggressive
when whatever passes for their blood is up.
I don't like to kill anything, deadly or not,
but I draw a line at my thresholds:
any such neighbour that crosses them
might be neighbour no more.
Perhaps the best that you can say
is that funnel-webs keep red backs away,
though very few others: certainly not the wolf spiders
who riddle our lawn with their burrows
and can be seen out hunting at night,
their emerald eyes glinting in torchlight,
or the St Andrew's Cross, with its great wide
web outside the back door, my
almost favourite, so
perfect the X it makes of itself, right
at the centre, like a man spread-
eagled in the middle of his being
or a ski-jumper at the top of her flight, second only
to the mystic orb-spider whose intricate tracery
between the wormwood and the lemon tree
is such a metaphor for poetry.
And yet there are more – the daddy-long-legs, say,
supposedly most poisonous of all
were it ever able to get fangs through skin

or the tiny, tentative swimmer I found in
the bathroom sink last winter, who stayed
three days or so, savouring the splash
of surf, the waves, thirsty beyond measure
for something I suspect there is no measuring,
or those other two, internal and, I guess, my
point in writing this: the one
whose web you see only on the MRI, the neat
bundles of its victims at C2 or 3 (you
never see the spider itself, but feel it, late at night,
testing the guy-ropes, patrolling
the trip-wires, tugging here and there where
something on a nerve needs tightening), and
this last one, stranger still,
whose web's his life itself: damaged
and torn, repaired a hundred times, ob-
ssessive beyond imagining, he'll
lumber out at almost any trouble or
excitement in his neighbourhood,
wrap it clumsily in a
cocoon of words, as if he thought it could
be kept, or understood.

Disabled Poem

Four friends have called in the last two days
from London, Perth, Canberra, Corowa,
and all quite unexpectedly.
They worry about me, they say, and need to know how I am.
I've heard from none of them for months
and am touched, of course,
but the synchronicity unsettles me – some
ghost-in-the-works, maybe, or
mood passing over; not, hopefully, a
portent of imminent disaster. *I'm*
alright, I say, *feeling*
fitter every day, ribs
healed at last, no
fall for months, mood
as good as it could be on this bright, high-
winded mountain Tuesday with
Trump and Clinton engaged in their first
Presidential debate, the world
hinged on a button, the only concept of a
keeping of the peace relentless war. *I'm*
fine, I tell them, walking
suddenly more carefully, *no*
new lesions and it's
all relative anyway, saying
nothing of the ancient, un-
shiftable dismay – *no*
plans to turn into an un-
papered Hispano-American or
Eritrean refugee or
child on the streets of Aleppo, become
an Indigenous
Australian on the streets of Darwin, let alone
shark off Ballina or
kangaroo in the parks of Canberra,

or dairy cow, pig
on an industrial farm,
battery chicken,
sheep…

'CREEPING UP ON THE THINGS THAT MATTER'

SID LARWILL

Twenty-two years ago, my wife became acutely ill with what was later diagnosed as CFS/ME. Taking sharing life's journey to an extreme, I became ill a year later, and was subsequently given the same diagnosis. It's not infectious. Just lucky I guess. What's mine is yours.

I never went back to work full-time and for the last fourteen years have been unable to work at all. Nature hates a vacuum and life has filled the space. Illness pushed us out of the mainstream. We became observers more than participants. Over a number of painful years I learned how much my sense of purpose and meaning in life was tied to my work life and career. I've had to find other things to pin my sense of being to – not always with success.

We moved to the country because life in the city was unsustainable for us. Both being ill has presented challenges. But we have a great deal to be thankful for. We have two boys, both still school age, and we live in a terrific community. We have enjoyed loads of support from our families and our friends. And we have each other.

It's true that when I first became ill I came close to committing murder. Well-meaning people told me that I would learn some life lessons, or that positives would come from it, or that when one door closes another opens. An overdeveloped sense of politeness stayed my hand and saved the lives of many. But now, looking back, I find myself thinking the same things, wanting to console others with the same platitudes. But they only mean something if you're there. And to give such advice unsolicited is to risk attack. So I hold my peace.

Of course, like anyone with chronic illness, at least to begin with, I searched and hoped for cures and recovery, investing a lot of money and emotional yearning into the process. Some of it has been good, great even. A lot of it has been crap. The alternative health practitioner who smilingly promised me in 1998 that I would be completely well in six weeks remains on the top of my homicidal wish list. Of course, now that this is in print,

I can never hope to kill the guy without prosecution; another life goal to strike off the list.

It is only in recent years that I have begun to realise that twenty years of hoping for recovery might start to look like delusion. And to always live in the shadow of how my life might be if I were well is to live a kind of suspended half-life. Because actually, when I looked at it, I discovered my life was beautiful. Not that I looked at it like that often, but it was nice when it happened. I realised it was better to reconcile myself to a life of chronic illness, that is to give up on the idea of recovery, and then to live that life well and with a sense of deep gratitude. So, 'If I were well again...' is a phrase I have banished from my lexicon.

Ironically, just as I got to a place of acceptance of a full life lived with illness, my wife over recent months has achieved a complete recovery (selfish wench!). To the outside eye the change appears miraculous, but it is the fruit of years of work combined with a new therapeutic method. Astounded, I find I now have to admit, again, the possibility of recovery myself. If it's possible for her then why not for me? Everything changes.

I began writing poetry over the last few years. It has allowed me to give voice to things that could have life in no other form – things that won't brook direct examination but which must be approached quietly, almost secretively, as if looking at them only vaguely from the corner of your eye, at the limit of your field of vision. I've had to creep up on the things that matter.

Blade of Grass

You compare me to a blade of grass.

Don't.

Yes, I know
it bends in the wind
and when the violence passes
it stands and is not broken.
It holds its tiny seeds aloft
giving of itself for their fattening
and only when all else is dry
lets them fall,
when all seems dead and gone,
to rock hard soil
and then resprouts with the first autumn rain.
Tiny overnight shoots of life.
Such resilience.
Such humility.
Such isness in its common place.
I know.
But don't compare me to a blade of grass.
I want to be something bigger, something stronger.
Always.
Compare me to a Red Gum
standing by a slothful river
casting shade over deeper pools.
A tree with girth
with centuries of living written into gnarly bark
canoe scars
or gaping maws from forest fires
with a trunk patched and hollow from years of standing
holding in its dead heart a family of Sugar Gliders
or a pair of Cockatoos.

Or compare me to an Oak tree
with shade enough to host a feast

for twenty on a burning Christmas day,
and a carpet of acorns
enough to beget a whole forest of trees
year
after year
after year.
Let me be green and fecund
dropping autumn leaves in thick abundance,
and in spring, springing huge leaves of green,
holding memories of generations of children climbing
to make secret private places in my embrace.
Standing like some ancient thing
on ancient ground
over a grand yard full of family history,
or a church
or a school ground
bells and kids' laughter caught daily in my leaves.

I know, I know.
We can't all be something grand.
And there is wisdom, sure,
in just being.
But a blade of grass?
A blade of grass?
I'm not ready or big enough for that,
that humble timelessness,
that invisibility.
You understand
all this time
I imagined I was taller
and I confess
there is little comfort in realising
I'm just an herbaceous border.

....

How to be Invalids Together: A Manifesto

Love.
And be loved.

Expect nothing. And wait.
Cherish what comes.

When she falls, stand strong.
When you fall, rest.

Be aware of the need to achieve, to be seen.
Be content then to achieve nothing, to be unseen.

Open your heart to the blessings of small things.
Sing their praises, in word, in being.

In a world that is always moving, be still.
In a world that is always making noise, be silent.

Love.
And be loved.

From Wood to Bliss

I...
I have a chook called Gutsy,
who's first to find the new grub,
hopping on the wheelbarrow,
kicking at a new-turned sod,
scratching at fresh rakings,
waiting expectantly at my feet.
The other chooks haven't half her gumption –
yes gumption –
they're onlookers.

I...
I showed my boy how to use an empty coke bottle as a kick board –
coke bottle kick board held secret in the depths,
lean legs kicking with quick ready joy.
I floated on my back and watched the storm clouds brewing.
I saw the first big drops,
caught the last of their long fall slap-splashing on my cheeks.
My sons jumped as electric bolts exploded,
and we drove home wet and laughing,
big drops smacking in through open windows.

I...
I sat on a granite outcrop,
vast vista spread before me.
A skink crawled from the fringing growth,
curiosity getting the better of fear
and sat with me awhile,
head tilted, watchful,
spiny bronze back half hidden in dappled shade.
We shared it.
The skink, my sandwich, and me.
A falcon cut the air below us,
swept up in an arc
and disappeared into the steely branches of a radio tower.
Always in a hurry on the wing.

Falcons.

I am not always like this –
not by any stretch –
this…bliss.
I can't help looking elsewhere
to poison myself with envy
of career paths and success,
of recognisability,
of easy fit,
of certainty,
of security,
of material comfort.
I like to mock them –
neat together designer lifestyles unfolding
to a Harvey Norman jingle.
But because of my envy,
I admit,
it's they who mock me.
The poison creeps and seeps.
My body petrifies,
becomes wood.

How do I transform?
From wood.
To bliss.
Somewhere in my heart I know.
I need to not only theorise, conjecture,
but know – really know –
read Tolstoy again;
read Dostoevsky –
know that history is illusion,
the grand narrative a construct,
heroic exploits ephemera.
Life's measure is in its fidelity to a labour of love,
not on a grand scale,
but in attendance to the smallest particulars,

abiding in a vulnerable localised care[38] –
this moment's shepherd.

That's my calling
if only I hear it.
This moment's shepherd.

I…
I sit in the still dusk with my love.
There's a gecko in the foliage of the quince tree.
We hear him climb, leaf to leaf.
Who knows?
Maybe tomorrow I'll hear the footfalls of a spider scurrying.
From wood.
To bliss.

....

38 In his discussion of *The Devils* by Dostoevsky, Rowan Williams writes of the
character Shatov: '(His) injunction to work…is (to) the labour of conserving life in
small particulars, a commitment to human history not as a grand project but as the
continuance of a vulnerable localised care.' R. Williams, *Dostoevsky: Language, Faith
and Fiction,* London: Continuum, 2008.

'TWO MINUS ONE = ZERO'

GRETTA JADE MITCHELL

It all began with the collapse of my lover. Just over three years ago now. I, a weeping witness raging with helplessness, with hopelessness, remain haunted by that day, by those numbers: 10.12.12. From this sequence of digits, other numerals began to rule my days and nights: 000; 38°C; –1; 3-day cycle; 10 mg – etc., etc. And yet, simultaneously, I lost count, lost count of everything.

How many nights had she been in High Dependency? How many mornings had I woken alone? How many cigarettes before the 8 am doctors' rounds are too many? How many whispers? How many hours would she still be alive? How many deaths had we already suffered?

So, I held on to numbers like a traumatised child learning to count, for words had collapsed with her, bleeding in a saltless, tumescent seizure. Words like *I am a full-time carer of a palliative care patient, and the writing of this submission identifies with metastatic cancer.* Words lost poetry.[39]

Needless to say, I lost count of how many times I heard, 'I don't know what to say. I don't know what to say. I don't know what to say. I don't know what to say.' Needless to say, I never heard those words from her.

Vulnerability magnifies, she says. (Or is multiplied, I concur.) The myth of the weakest as target is reality, she says. People wish you dead, she says.

---

39 Even my dictionary lost pages, a glaring lacuna, a blank of missing pages from Poe-like, *adj.* to po-face, *n.* faced me mercilessly:
   and the syntax of linguistics majors. God, I'm lost to science.
   and the victory song of footballers. God, I'm lost to culture.
   and the zero-below rhyming of signs. God, I'm lost to life.
   masturbating third-rate journalese (they know their Latin and they speak with lisps). God, I'm lost to money.
   and the blunt and coded tech-talk of love. God, I'm lost to sex.
   and the theft of lines, inferior to mine. God, I'm lost to writing.
   and the forced tears of postmodernists. God, I'm lost to pathos.
   and the will to live as spite and irony. God, I'm lost to loss.

Take your family, Gretta. They wanted me – the sick person – to die. (The dying must die! says I.) And became angry when that didn't happen, says she.

Illness is a misogynistic hierarchy, she says. A woman suffering will be told there is a man suffering more than she. At risk, the sick and the infirm require non-competitive spaces, she says. Because we are non-competitive creatures, she says. (Never confuse humility with mediocrity, I concur.) Plants, she says. For the terminally ill and scared, she says. Lying down, propped up watching TV with a loved one, a trusted one, holding hands is a blessed act.

Michelle, I love you. I have lost count of all we have lost.

Untitled Verse of Pain

In bed with textas, journal, blank A6
Among other things

Fine, acute pages only I may see
Among other things

And neutropoenic – send no flowers' bloom
Among other things

Our mothers cursed us, 'enfant terribles!'
Among other things

They're vindicated now she's dying young
Among other things

Don't speak! The future is forbidden here
Among other things

Her bedside killers: 10 mg at will
Among other things

I hand her folded poems on paper black
Among other things

And want her ghost to scare my library
Among other things

And when I'm dreaming she is absent space
Among other things

A funny dance to make her laugh despite
Among other things

I am her only, only ~~family~~
Among other things

Researching suicide in bed. Her move
Among other things

What will become, become, of me, of me?
Among other things

I turn to God, but God he hates me still
Among other things

Around the hospital, I know my way
Among other things

Collapse, collapse, collapse, collapse, collapse
Among other things

She's lost all int'rest in performance stats
Among other things

Cold winter front in city, city streets
Among other things

The whims of ugly kin, deserted us
Among other things

– neglect! Abuse her through the final days
Among other things

We are the product of addiction mass
Among other things

She gives me kisses in the morning sun
Among other things

And Death is *not* an abstract concept, son
And Death is *not* an abstract concept, son

Sonnet to Delete

– None of this exists tonight; just tracks
Of letters and of paint. (Her hard refuge,
The truth of hate.) Come down at last, collapse
The traps, the tests, the reading needles' bruise.

Elsewhere they'd kiss her dying eyes, elsewhere
They'd *danse* with death – of vigils, criminal;
Of power, circling beds of prey. It's there
Antigone's lost fight belongs. We brawl.

– None of this exists tonight; we dance
Like sprites of ghetto daze. Slow motion clues
Like love delayed, the friends of Necromance.
Disease don't care; and Death cheats all the rules.

Survival is a couplet turn, the day
They want you off the books — — — —

I'm Reading Her Journal and I Wish To Be Deaf
Or, Another Test...

I lie awake, eyes open to the dark and listen;
      she's breathing.
It's a fail-proof death test.
Listening hard, the indifferent emptiness says,
      she's not here.
I hear her breath, her breath, and wish to be deaf.

*

13 pairs of reference headphones I've destroyed this past year. 50 mm drivers are my preference. It's like wearing small speakers on your ears and they don't blow-up easy – it takes a pretty hellish playlist, at a pretty hellish volume. Even then, destruction's not guaranteed.

I confess I assumed that as I went deaf I would be blessed with an encroaching nothingness: silence, complete and catatonic. Just as I presume the blind see nothing, I had presumed that the deaf hear nothing. I've been wrong before and I'll be wrong again. In surdity, I'm exposed to a sonic plenum.

I can't hear the sound of a match falling on polished floorboards, no; I can't distinguish certain speech sounds from others, no; but, I hear the high-pitched whistling of imaginary trains rolling through the post-industrial night; I hear mechanical pterodactyls screaming in mid-air death-fights; I hear jackhammers grinding acres of glass; I hear ghost dogs howling, dead babies crying. I hear her breathing when I'm sleeping alone.

There was a time when phonoreception was precious to me. And I listened, I listened hard. As engineer of a new wave, a new sound, my ears were an underground treasure. (Now there's a paradoxical tautology, if ever I heard one.) Recording EPs for depressed teenagers who danced alone at beach parties, neck-deep in anthems of loss…that's when I met her. Years ago, years before adolescents were patriotic and happy. Or, worse – energetic. All this 110% crap makes me want to retch. I miss apathy on the faces of our youth, neglected and poor. Like hers.

She's requested her journal. As I pack for the hospital, I read:

People ask me if I'm superstitious. My stock answer is: *I try not to be.* I don't say I avoid the number 13. Like when the volume on my stereo hits 13, it makes me uncomfortable and I quickly adjust it. Or when I see an image of an owl and look away with a start, because an Aboriginal friend once said an owl means someone close will die – means death is on its way.

In 2013, I was diagnosed with cancer. It was also the year of my 13th anniversary with Gretta. I realise now when you make a wish it's important to add a few clauses.

I would often think it'd be great for someone to write about my life.

Gretta writes about my life. (But my wish was missing the clause – that I should not be terminally ill.)

I don't make wishes anymore. If I do, it's that *all things stay exactly as they are*. I don't want anything to change.

Most people love to catch others' contradictions. I know I do. Once in a palliative care appointment, I made it known that I don't (and try not to) think of the future. A few moments later, regarding taking certain medications, I said: *Maybe, in the future.* The specialist jumped on me saying: *Future?* Pleased to catch my contradiction, she, like all doctors, think they are smart. I said: *Yeah, I don't know. In the future. Like on my D—Bed.*

Saying the *D* word makes me cringe. And I can't seem to write it either. The *D* word, that is. When I read the word *cancel*, I automatically think of *cancer*. Doctors could say *cancel* instead of *cancer*. Cancel your life. Cancel whatever you were doing. Cancel your future. Cancel your hopes and dreams, your likes and dislikes. Cancel your attitude. But don't cancel your past, because your past is – or could be – the reason for the word *cancer* today. Cancel witticisms, ideas, inventions, perceptions, the ability to read the world. Cancel social satire. The vanity of which is red-faced in the pale of mortality. Cancel music, fashion, cool records, cool shoes, flash phones, mansions, credit, status, income. Cancel talent; cancel intelligence.

Fading rapidly, they don't matter.

What matters?

– to be pain free.

Not feeling nauseated. Warmth. Or coolness when it's hot. Love. Love. Love. Quiet company. Love. Understanding. Holding hands with your lover. Her soft, warm, sometimes cool, hands. Hearing her breathe at night. The sight of her cute feet in socks. Calmly watching crappy TV with a friend.

Two years ago I was told I had six months to live. We were living in Adelaide, making a life for ourselves. I decided that it would be best for Gretta to be surrounded by her family, who live in Brisbane, when I passed.

I thought, *I will do this final selfless act for her.* We moved to Brisbane to live with her sister and her sister's partner (male) and two sons. It was a complete disaster. After two years of solid heckling and harassment from the eldest son – face-pulling and eye-rolling from the adults – we made it back to Adelaide.

Soon after my diagnosis I'd thought that I had learnt all of life's lessons.

I was wrong.

Of course.

Lesson 1. People do not change just because they know you are dying. (Although, there will be a short reprieve from whatever bullshit they've subjected you to – because, let's face it, nobody wants the fact that they were a complete arsehole to you, for no apparent reason, when you were well, on their conscience. So, they will come running to your bedside in an attempt to save their own souls.)

Lesson 2. Never be selfless. (It's dangerous for you and your loved ones. It's not righteous or noble.)

Lesson 3. People can and will use your illness against you. (They will insinuate you are addicted to drugs, when all you are doing is taking the medication prescribed by specialists. They will say the drugs are affecting your behaviour when you don't behave according to the whims of their moods. It goes without saying: *avoid contact with such people.*)

Lesson 4. People will resent you for not working. (Even though you are terminally ill and on the disability pension.)

Lesson 5. Some folks believe cancer is contagious. (True.)

Lesson 6. It is common to meet oncologist registrars who think that for a woman to lose her hair is worse than the cancer itself. And, everyone in the ward thinks seeing the patient's hair regrow is the best possible outcome. (People don't like reminders that African Americans [slaves] built America's first railroad system. And everyone thinks that an African American doctor is the best possible outcome.)

Lesson 7. Never assume you will receive mercy. (Never.)

'ACHE'S INTERVAL'

KEVIN GILLAM

My poems are written with the underlying history and ongoing treatment of my condition known as acromegaly. This disease is quite rare (3–5 per million) and is caused by a pituitary tumour which leaks growth hormone. I have had this disease since the age of seventeen, but was not diagnosed until aged twenty-two. The major symptoms include overgrowth of head, jaw, hands and feet, increased hunger and sleepiness, sweating, darkening of skin colour, changes to facial and body structure, arthritis, diabetes and general lethargy. I have had numerous operations, including two brain tumour resections, both hips replaced, both shoulders replaced, both elbows operated upon, gall bladder removed, spinal surgeries and radiotherapy on the brain. My current treatment involves taking a large number of prescription drugs for replacing and controlling hormone functions and injecting a drug known as octreotide into my stomach three times a day. This drug regulates growth hormone in the body. Without treatment, sufferers of acromegaly continue to gain bone and body weight whilst the heart remains at the same size. This results in a severely reduced life span.

My poems, 'propped' and '(not enough words for those to be tongued)', both deal with the medical realm and encounters but are written from different perspectives. The poem 'propped' is deliberately fragmented in structure with four syllables per line. The third-person voice describes the thoughts of a person in a hospital bed – 'plas / tic beneath sheet' – as he/she thinks back over days past whilst the interruptions and necessities of the hospital routine – 'cuff, swab' – are played out. In between these lines, those in italics – *'listen to that / augmented fourth / ache's interval / resolving in / into unrhyme / resolving out / to scree of now'* – depict both the whispers of now and of fate. In writing this and other poems I am conscious of making reference to as many senses as possible, hence the lines 'smell / of wet earth' and 'night / nurse moth.' The use of touch and smell are primary to the link between text and reader.

The poem '(not enough words for those to be tongued)' describes the mental state of someone approaching a crucial medical appointment. The text is fragmented into three line stanzas, each with a syllable count of 6/1/6. This assists in invoking the fraught state of mind and anxiety felt as the time of appointment approaches. The poetic 'voice' asks the patient to surrender to the moment – 'you // as flotsam, tossed, pikefish, / one / eye away from weed.' And the penultimate line – 'door // begins, he opens.' – changes the normal wording so as to further enhance apprehension.

These poem are typical of my style in terms of a strict adherence to form and use of sensory detail. They also attempt to address the state of mind of the patient and the thoughts invoked in the medical encounter, issues not normally raised by professionals in the area.

'clockwise is off'

in this convalescence – good word that with its
gauze-like length and syllabic wrap – been

practising that lost art of waiting, bus and
train stations, doctors' rooms, never enough

shade or new 'New Ideas', been watching,
the wizened and the upright, figs ripening,

footpaths that flow like prose then trip like
misspellings, been rubbing paperbark trees,

listening in on frogs, been mulling over the
difference between learned and remembered,

the venn intersects, making a mantra
of 'clockwise is off' while pondering the

origin of knowns, the mind that did
the choosing, hands that shape our days

....
propped

in the dia
ry of clean be
ginnings. gift of
ponder? you make
an entry. plas
tic beneath sheet.
listen to that
a line about
clouds. absent but
near? dialect
of cirrus. night
nurse moth. how
light goes sepi
a before rain.
beyond index.
augmented fourth
remembering.
ache's interval
hovers. the smell
of wet earth. all
your yesterdays.
resolving in
songs of loose pick
ets. heelless. how
the wind stole your
stories. slapping.
into unrhyme
sold them elsewhere.
cuff, swab. then lat
er. memory's
pylons. much lat
er. fluky veins.
resolving out
how you find your
self. drips. stooped ov
er. neap tide. lap

ping at these same
lines. feeding you.
to scree of now
from a vast un
mapped. inland sea

....
(not enough words for those to be tongued)

so you're better tonight
but
read better as bandaged

and you've had instincts of
nine,
two bars plus fermata,

but as you ascend the
bricked
serendipity of

the blind you begin to
fear
what the morrow might bring.

so see it as a jour-
ney
down the fingerboard of

'cello, from middle C
to
aural stratosphere, hear

it as the primaeval
wash
of chords i to vi, you

as flotsam, tossed, pikefish,
one
eye away from weed. for

now, collapse into this
temp-
orary place of ease.

what hovers? velour wait-
ing
room, lino moment. door

begins, he opens. in
breath,
'your scans, yes, they've come back'

'THE CONDITION'

RACHAEL GUY

*Bodies do not produce sensations, but complexes of
elements (complexes of sensations) make up bodies.*
– Ernst Mach, The Analysis of Sensations (1902)

If you met me you wouldn't know that I live with a debilitating condition.

I belong to a category of individuals who don't fit neatly into medical classifications and who often fail to fulfil preconceptions about what 'chronic illness' looks like.

I was born with a hypersensitivity to pain and highly mobile joints. My childhood memories are a synesthetic map of bodily and emotional discomfort. I recall being averse to smells, sense impressions, noise and bodily sensation. There was always some part of my body inexplicably in pain and I experienced intense mood fluctuations as a result. A lifelong insomniac, I remember solitary nights of chronic leg pain or fitful waking after nightmares. The very walls of my room seemed to ache in unison with my small body, the wallpaper oozing foreboding and nausea.

Growing up, I was intense, highly emotional and marginal amongst my peers.

In primary school, I was quick-witted and could contort my highly flexible body into disconcerting shapes – a trick which could bring the classroom to a standstill and afford me a moment of transitory credibility with the other children. Although I was curious and boisterous, pain always had a way of hijacking my attention and dragging me away into dark and melancholy rumination. Pain interrupted my learning.

As an adult, nothing much has changed; depression is always just beneath the surface and I grapple with widespread musculoskeletal pain on a daily basis. I am frequently fatigued and overwhelmed by sensory input, and have dramatic mood fluctuations. I experience problems with loose hyper-flexible joints and spasming muscles. My homeostasis is extremely fragile and my body consumes a lot of energy just maintaining equilibrium. These bodily traits have had ramifications on my ability to work, socialise and be at ease in the world.

So what exactly is my 'condition'? It has been hard to find a label, impossible to separate the psychological from the tightly intertwined physical. For a time fibromyalgia and clinical depression were the closest I had to a satisfactory diagnosis. More recently I was informed that the real culprit is joint hypermobility syndrome (JHS) with dysautonomia (a term for the disregulation of the autonomic nervous system which affects basic bodily functions, such as sleep, heart rate, digestion etc.). Joint hypermobility sounds benign enough, but for a small percentage of people it can be a chronically disabling condition with widespread manifestations throughout the body. When it was raised as a diagnosis, the whole spectrum of my suffering suddenly made sense as aspects of a 'syndrome'. My symptoms are not a random scattering of singular, unrelated bodily events – they belong to a specific constellation.

It has been a long journey to reach this point of understanding. Over the years, I have eddied around myriad medical professionals seeking an explanation as new and confounding symptoms presented. But it has been akin to chasing ghosts around an infinite maze. Over time, I have become increasingly frustrated with the vagueness and disorientation of conflicting diagnoses. Perhaps the most enigmatic explanation I received was from a rheumatologist who simply said: 'There is the illusion of pain – but there is *no pain*.'

All too often I've been met with hostility and dismissal, as another specialist has conceded that they haven't encountered anything quite like it – or have tried to pigeonhole my symptoms into their 'pet syndrome', leading to inappropriate and disheartening treatment regimes.

I sympathise with people who have conditions that aren't easy to categorise.

We perplex, confound and unsettle. It can take years to find answers. In both daily life and in the clinic we find ourselves faced with the gruelling and repetitive task of having to describe our symptoms again and again to relative strangers. There is an essential ambivalence about being forced to call up the attendance roll of physical ills over and over. It is a painful disclosure, in some ways re-traumatising – certainly immensely vulnerable. It has a limiting effect on self-esteem and is, quite frankly, like obsessively picking at an open wound.

I am sick of the words 'highly unusual', 'hypersensitive', 'atypical', 'abnormal' and 'rare.' They can come to feel like they subtly imply notions like 'non-compliant', 'hysterical' and 'neurotic'. 'It's all in your head' seems to be the underlying assumption and antidepressants are invariably the first line of treatment offered. Antidepressants have occasionally been helpful, but more often harmful.

This language of incomprehension pushes me back into a space of unknowing and can have the effect of devaluing the subjective experience of living with the symptoms. It's highly isolating. When you live with bodily instability and unpredictability, it is hard to move through the world with assuredness and consistency – and when there is seemingly no name for your experience, self-doubt can plague you.

As I have grappled with the peculiar aloneness of living with 'invisible disability', writing has emerged as a place of refuge. During the long and often fruitless search for diagnostic words that made sense of my lived condition, I instead found my own poetic language. Language has helped me make sense of desolate places of intense frustration and alienation. Through language, I have been able to find the poetry and absurdity of my bodily dissonance. I can divert my attention away from the persistent white noise of my central nervous system and arrive at a place of acceptance. When I have felt stranded between 'normality' and 'abnormality', or submerged beneath a new wave of pain, I have turned to words to make my own meaning and find consolation. Writing does not offer transcendence from suffering but is a way of facing 'what is'. Writing offers a space in which to invite others to converse, convene and perhaps gain new insights into the diversity of embodied experience.

Through poetry I am finding the *particular* language for my 'atypical' body – I am writing my way out of isolation and into dialogue with others, my embodied experience and the world. Through the written word, I give voice to the discord, ambivalence, inconvenience, fear and beauty of this corporeal existence.

Discontinuation

1. The mind I've grown into over five medicated years is being disassembled. A woolly dreadfulness descends, nausea and bone-breaking fatigue. I'm submerged in a space between sanity and something unruly, inchoate.

2. Setting out, I am dimly aware of a sensation in my head, a storm brewing. The streets are uncannily still and empty, yet objects keep appearing abruptly and inexplicably. Walking, I stumble into pedestrians who loom into my vision, ghost ships emerging out of fog. A car hurtles into view, as if out of nowhere. Birds and dogs topple momentarily into sight and are gone.

3. Pulling out of an intersection, I narrowly escape a head-on collision. I look left, right, right, left – all about me a crisp, reverberating emptiness. Coasting forward, I barely miss another car. At that moment I realise the landscape is not in fact

4. *empty* – it's just that I   can't *see*

5. I am in effect   *blind*   to anything   in   transit. My world,
   a theatre set   caught in the hush before opening,   the scenography
   hinting at what is to come,   while the actors go unseen.
   Somewhere   en route between seeing and perceiving   the
   message is   getting

6. lost.

7. I pull over at a roadside amenities block. Shaken, I sit down in a cubicle, press the heels of my hands into my eyelids. I am trying to find reality amidst the neurological white noise of glitches and static. Suddenly there comes a sound leaching through the walls – oppressive, guttural, seeping. Am I going insane?

8. Quivering, I step outside. Before me, a huge truck, bulging with pigs, rising tier upon tier. Their snouts and pink-scabbed eyes push through

bars – they reek of filth, hot distress, slurry of shit. Scream. Scream. Scream.

9. 'Christ', I think, 'Truth is stranger than...'

10. Crying/laughing. Crying/laughing.   Aching/confusion.   Elation/ anger. Crying/laughing/crying/laughing.   Crying.

11. The thoughts of others are contagious. Their demeanours are sticky and penetrating. I am so porous that I become their words, their gestures. My self, [no-self] is an echo chamber for external narratives, a mirror reflecting fragments.

12. I have pulled my thumb from the pharmaceutical dyke. My brain is in flood. Language, the raft I cling to, disintegrates.   I drift.

13. At the supermarket checkout, I glance down at my wallet. Scrabbling amongst small change, another person's hands.

14. They move of their own volition and are twenty years older than the rest of my body. I watch as skin crawls up my wrists, another person's arms colonising my sleeves. The phantom body grows quickly – dermis rises to cover my face, a prickling, incoming flesh-tide. Hair follicles break through my scalp, a posture, and demeanour emerge, *not my own*. I am vanishing; find myself speechless, encased within a body within a body.

15. My mind has succumbed to a strange docility. Arms and legs swim in a semblance of co-ordination. I can hold no thoughts. They pool like stagnant air at the edges of my awareness, inarticulate and irretrievable.

16. Time has no shape – to walk the length of a street takes aeons. Everything pulses with a kind of vitalism. The plane trees wear growth's trajectory upon their pallid forms, limbs singing its bruisings and distortions. I lay my hand on one and can identify no distinction between my own skin and the mottled bark.

17. Today, simple things. I drink tea from a yellow cup and make toast.

18. Dusk. Out walking, seeds and insects topple towards me as meteorites. They snag in my hair and catch in my eyelashes. Roses along a fence line frighten with their tumescence and colour. The jumping spider's spinnerets fidget like huge weavers' hands. The line it spins cleaves the evening open in its wake.

19. Tonight,
       the black of the road
              swallows me –
                      its substance,
                              like death,
                  an unstoppable
              river of pitch
          nothingness
              insinuating its way
                  upwards into my
                              eyes
                     my body,
                  smaller
            with each step –
      my lurching heart
    each
        trembling breath
            lodged
           deeply,
              inexorably
          within

          its tarry mass.

20. I'm putting everything down now. I just can't anymore.

21. Please just leave me.   Alone.

22. The garden is my solace; I have used every square inch to stave off madness. It is bulging with verdant determination. Weeds, flowers, fruit and rot mingle. I am running out of space.

23. Sleepless. Nothing stops the revulsion I feel towards my own bed, the cloying grip of pillow, tangle of sheet. All day I hanker for sleep, and then when I get there

24. ——

25. Insomnia. A million regrets raining down at dawn. Like iron filings they cling, my grief a magnet.

26. Why can I sleep in other people's houses, but not my own? In other houses, sleep becomes a gentle duty, perhaps an act of conviviality. The pre-sleep mind encompasses all those other bodies, slumbering in unfamiliar rooms. Each of us dreaming; the night house, a creaturely burrow. The consolation of collective aloneness.

27. (Nothing.)

28. A small shade of blue awaiting dissolution.

29. Public transport. Looking directly at other people terrifies me. Their lurid humanity is too big to apprehend at a glance. Their eyes are piercing, the mobile seams of their mouths, unpredictable. A quaking begins to rise in my body. I exit.

30. Must I live a life –

31. shut away in rooms of my own making? Most days I dream of escape. Most days, I get no further than the front door.

32. Life is a protracted goodbye. A slow and incremental withdrawal.

33. I watch a film about a woman living a life of voluntary simplicity. A cabin in the woods, whitewashed hearth. When asked if she wants for anything she says: 'Nothing. I think I've been saying "no" to things all my life.'

34. ...I've been saying 'yes[no]'   all my life.

35. I often cry beside rivers. I cry too under trees and on mountains, lost to the vastness of the sky. I am comforted by the disquieting presence of the gigantic and the miniscule. The grief I feel for the living and dead is spacious, irrefutable.

36. Each morning I wake to the small calamity of self. Light and sound are sharp; I squint and hug the shadows. My new unmedicated mind is jittery, unreliable and passionless. It is capricious; it waxes between making sense and creating unreliable narratives about existence. But perhaps this is all we have.

37. Comes a burgeoning calm, soft and clear.

38. The sea rolls in, rolls out,   my breath rises and falls.

....

Hyper [sensitive]

As if my very matter was in argument
with itself – my senses verge on intolerable.

Within this skin everything is on
a spectrum of discomfort –

I smell the fetid underlying nuance
of all things, teeter at the edge of nausea.

My feet throb, recalling the ground,
sound shatters my attention.

Joints drift from sockets, my sternum
quietly unzips itself in the night.

Vertebrae pop and scrape as I mobilise
this assemblage I call my body.

In sunlight the capillaries' high-pitched
howl crackles beneath my cheeks.

Water leaves me burning. Textures
overwhelm.

Sleepless again, the weight of my
body assumes a detestable ache.

I have longed for soft sensorial places
but found no refuge.

My skin winces at contact as if the world
and others in it were to be endured.

Discordant song of my becoming –
are you the kink in my proprioception?

Come night, the heart once again
hammers out its arrhythmic nocturne.

Climacteric

Tossed in the amniotic slick
of life's mid-line, memory scuttles,
myopic as a beetle in a jar.

Words spill from the mouth
like riders thrown from the saddle.
Muscles freeze – skin is threadbare.

Vitality becomes a thin curtain
trailing in an empty window.
All that once made me
is being unpicked.

Form collapses softly –
seams comes apart –
the pocket and pleat,
selvedge and ruching.

Jung said,
'in the secret hour of life's midday
death is born...'

No longer at the summit
we advance towards the valley
where the ascent
began.

'STRENGTH FROM WRITING'

GRANT COCHRANE

'And where does pain go, he wondered, when it goes away?
Does it disappear, or does it go somewhere else? I know, he thought.
It goes into the well of your weakness; and it waits.'
– Martin Amis, The Pregnant Widow

In my twenties I had a boring public service career, and in my thirties I decided to relieve the boredom with some mature age study. I was interested in linguistics and history; almost as an afterthought I took a unit in archaeology. After one semester I was hooked. I eventually got my honours degree in archaeology, then spent three years in South Africa doing my PhD. By the time I felt like a qualified archaeologist, I was well into my forties.

Then my body betrayed me.

There were times in South Africa when I would go to stand and found that I couldn't straighten up. I thought it was a bit comical, and put it down to too much sedentary study, not enough exercise. When I got back to Australia I mentioned it to a doctor and the X-rays showed I had a bit of osteoarthritis, nothing much to worry about. I started doing consulting work in the heritage management industry, conducting archaeological surveys and excavations with Aboriginal people. It was the kind of work I'd spent almost a decade training for, interesting but physically demanding.

After a few years, I found that the soreness was no longer just in my back. It was in my shoulders, hands, legs, feet; just about all my joints. I had a few other issues too – weird things going on with my digestive system. My platelet and white blood cell counts were extremely low, and my GP said he thought I might have Sjögren's syndrome. The rheumatologist didn't like labels, and said it was more accurate to think about a spectrum of autoimmune disorders and that I was somewhere on that spectrum. As are many people.

These conditions are potentially dangerous in the long term, but for me the immediate issue was arthritis. After a busy day at work I was finding that I couldn't get out of bed in the morning. If I used anti-inflammatories, my stomach would rebel violently. I gave away fieldwork and set up a consultancy specialising in lab-based analysis of artefacts, but there was no demand for that kind of work and I ended up losing a lot of money. I had to give archaeology away.

Which brings me to writing. After finishing high school, before embarking on my boring public service career, I used to write a bit and wondered if I could be a journalist. I tried for a couple of years to get a cadetship but when I failed, I gradually lost interest in writing. For some reason – maybe it's the vacuum left by losing my archaeological career, the fact that I have a lot more time for reading – I find myself writing poetry and short stories again. It feels different this time around, much more pleasurable.

Chronic pain is an interesting subject for a poet to work with. It touches on some of the big transcendental themes – mortality, fear, courage, empathy, the human spirit. For me, pain is mainly a source of frustration, definitely not just a physical thing. I hate that cleaning my own shower recess is a task that has to be deferred to a very good day. More disconcerting is the fact that those very good days are becoming fewer and fewer. But these are negative thoughts, and negativity is the ally of pain. Pain seems to feed upon it. Whenever I write a poem or a story that I am happy with – regardless of whether or not it gets published – all traces of negativity disappear for a while. So it's a therapeutic kind of pastime, and a fortifying one.

Even on Winter Days

There's an old mannequin
bobs up and down in the waters of my dreams.
It's hard to think of
a dummy in distress.
I prefer other interpretations.
It's cold, it's wet. It's seasonal. The late
autumn breezes creak through windows.
Limbs get pinned and needled. What comes goes.

Mooloolaba beach is patrolled
seven days per week, all year round.
Even on winter days, the sand is warm.
You can rest easy.
The waves carry nothing more than kelp.

...

The clock chimes ten and then eleven.
It is time for bed.
Eyes are tired, mind is wandering,
who could sew in this light?
Still, another cup is poured
and the tinkle of the sugary spoon
rouses that lazy cat
who sleeps in bubbles of immortal bliss.

....
Horizontal

and that is just
the first hour.
in fact hours
are the timeframe of pain –
the waking hour,
       the rehab hour,
the Jesus hour,
       the torture hour,
the footy show hour…

have you noticed, Mary,
second hands are usually red,
like emaciated fire engines –
bustling, self-important, flash.
look at that hour hand –
solid, resolute, imperceptible.
it knows all about half
lives and dignified decay.

when Beth came into the cosmos,
screaming as though struck by an ice sheet,
she had little concept of chronometrics,
just warmth tick ice
ice ice ice ice ice tick warmth.
there were hours of pain in that room,
then, abruptly,
the re-emergence of life beyond pain.

hours end –
sand in molten glass subsides
and in the upper chamber
a residue of grit abides.

Inkling

a gaunt jekyll posing to contemplate
on bent elbow and knee the bruised skin that
comes so easy to some in broken plates
sink further into the deep encasing

in the arthritic blue-tongue garden those
tails that used to frighten like grassless snakes
now have pet names seem to bend like mirrors
hidden in the skin shed out back of mind

the idea of no idea the
philosophy of abatement
filters in and out of the nails clinging
purposefully to this morning's dental

floss and hanging over head the perfect crime

'MY POLICY ON PROCEDURES'

ROB WALKER

My main condition is chronic osteoarthritis. I had a total knee replacement (TKR) in February 2015, although as I write this a year later it is still 'tight' and swells daily. I also have plantar fasciitis in both heels so walking for pleasure isn't an option at the moment. My stomach won't tolerate the anti-inflammatories any longer. I manage the pain with analgesics. The effect on my writing has been interesting. Knowing that I'd be practically immobile for a few months after the knee replacement I envisioned hours of free time to work on poetry, short stories or even the embryonic stages of a novel. The reality was quite different.

The operation went well but the pain continued week after week. Tramadol was the only painkiller I could tolerate, having experienced depression earlier with Endone. It dealt with the pain but filled my head with cotton wool – like being permanently drunk but not so much fun. It meant that I couldn't hold a thought for long, solve a complex problem or think tangentially. The work I planned was abandoned. Without the mental acuity, I couldn't create poetry (although I did 'dotpoint' sensations and experiences which later developed into poems like 'Coming off the Tramadol' and 'Who are you?' in *Policies & Procedures*). In the middle of all of this I was doing final edits for *tropeland* with the *Five Islands* editors in Melbourne by email. They were very patient with me. (Another side effect of the Tramadol was irritability. My initial response to most suggestions was to baulk: 'It's fine as it is' – but perhaps the preciousness on my part wasn't solely attributable to the medication!) Interestingly, I could still appreciate music and spent sleepless night hours re-listening to the discographies of Paul Simon and Joni Mitchell and daylight hours learning songs on the guitar for which I hadn't had time for years.

In time, I've returned to writing. I plan to travel more over the next few years and find ways to work around the reduced mobility. I published *Policies & Procedures* to get the 'ailment business' out of my system. I hope that my writing is generally optimistic and entertaining.

In any event, when I look at the chronic conditions with which many people live every day, my medical issues are minor. My general health is pretty good and the pain isn't such that it always needs to be reflected in my writing. I have no intention of letting the medical issues define me or my work!

....
radiology*

holding our future in nervous hands
we come with X-rays – ikons
in large envelopes with corporate logos

queue for the Delphic Oracle
who divines the auspices
like chook entrails

this arcane analysis
reading the stars within…

Under cold cathode lights, imaging replacing
ugly imagining our thoughts digitise into black
and white vaporising to harsh words

I would put those speech
bubbles under their own scan
break down the components of their diphthongs

meaning as signs reciprocally determined:
sick/well – a dichotomy sanctioned by the ticking clock,
nervous hands melting like Dali's

this arcane analysis,
internal astrology.

*Note: composed with Magdalena Ball.

....

extra-corporeal shockwave therapy

a wake-up call for the healing of my heels
a kind of ultrasound electrocution

the snappy crack brings back
Philip Glass's Lightning

you become acclimatised
to thumping pain

begin to think about
Yahia's torture in Iraq

wonder how you could ever
endure electrocution

without insanity

yet you slowly
become inured

and drift off into
a kind of reverie

where your foot
is on fire

....
endoscopy

i swallow the impossible.
meds perform their magic

i drift on dunlopillo clouds
so relaxed that nurses must

pat my face
give gentle orders

drift back on a dinghy
from a foreign country

to the first cries of a baby
in the labour ward next door

a new day begins for both of us

'BRAIN STORMS'

INDIA BREEN

I was 17 years old when I had my first seizure. Looking up into my mother's eyes I saw an absolute fear, wild within her face. She looked terror-stricken. Afraid *for* me and *of* me. She found me after she had been calling for a while and I hadn't replied. When she came to check in on me, there I was: unconscious, muscles contracting and blood running out of my mouth onto the carpet. I vaguely remember the ambulance coming and paramedics telling me to hop in the van, but I wouldn't, so Mum drove me to hospital. My mouth throbbed. I had bitten into a quarter of my tongue.

I woke up next to a Christmas tree in hospital with nurses asking me what year it was. My mouth was aching with a strong and steady rhythm. Mum was squeezing me too hard, telling me to 'Look at the Christmas tree!' but I didn't know what anything was. I stayed in hospital for the day and, several hours later, my memory started to return.

The only thing I couldn't remember was the seizure itself. I had asked my mother what I looked like and she'd told me I looked like thunder clapping the floor as my limbs slapped the ground. She demonstrated with her mouth clenched and her hands curled like lobster claws. It was a long and slow awakening – I felt before I saw, I tasted before I could hear, and the pain was as indistinguishable as the air around me. I suppose I first noticed my head; the fact that my mind felt separate from my brain.

In the years that followed, my mother stood by me as I trialled an assortment of medication and neurologists, each as unsuccessful as the other. The tablets caused forgetfulness, confusion, sleepiness, anxiety and depression. They were supposedly ceasing *all* electrical action inside my brain, which made my world uncoloured and created a black hole where I had previously filed my most important information. Almost every time I tried to access my intelligence and creativity, I was sent down a dense pathway of sprawling cobwebs. Still, to this day, I've never known what's made me more insecure – having a fit in public or not being able to state my ideas the way I used to.

I've cut a lot of things out of my life, mainly social things which demand drunkenness, and the people who used to invite me to such things. After my diagnosis, I witnessed faces glazing over and saw body language changing in a matter of moments, people literally unaware that epilepsy wasn't contagious. I feel those moments have pushed me into this tiny shell of shyness; even though I don't believe the stigma around my condition, I've seen it right in front of me. I know that my medication is filtered through my liver and I know that epilepsy is genetic. My main concern is that I will not have a liver when I am forty-three or that I will pass this burden onto my future children. I even worry that the condition itself will make me a confused and frazzled mother.

Although I haven't had a seizure for five years, I still have epilepsy. I'm better at managing it, but if I have less than eight hours sleep or even a smidgen of alcohol, my arms will twitch and my brain will smudge. It might not escalate to a grand mal seizure, but my mind anticipates them, so it leads me to a panic attack. I have spent almost a decade of my life in constant anticipation of having a seizure. During that time, I've noticed my one and only survival instinct has been to have a constant and acute awareness of how I *feel*. 'I *feel* weird' has been my living mantra, and it's left me isolated and powerless.

Seizures

I want to see my body make *thunder and sleep* –
my arms pleated, like foils ready to lift.
I want to dance on washed stones under coloured lights.
The jasmine, its invincible command, swaying with me,
and I, unsteady, clawing at the sky.
I want to swim in the pool's alloy, wrong.
I want to grip a balanced tray of iced beverages –
my hand suctioned like a star against the cold silver.

....
Giving up Ground

My last seizure I don't even remember.
Well, you don't remember them, of course,
but sometimes I got a sense something was wrong,
some thunder in my brain, rain in my hands,
a wobbly foot as though I'd trod on a loose paver.
It was very unlike all the others. I was shaving
my legs in the shower of a yacht just off St Tropez.
The moment my memory returns I see myself
wrapped in a towel standing on the deck.
It muddles again.
A small tender boat slapping over waves,
tiny specks of sea misting about my face.
A French doctor who seemed troubled by me.
Unknown medication in a ziplock plastic satchel.
A broken rib.
The looks I received from my colleagues back on the boat.
I've tried erasing from my mind the clink
of my razor on the stainless floor,
the rat-tat-tat of the anchor rolling in as we angled for shore.
They told me we were stopping for uniforms,
my friend picked me up from the dock.
You know my brain is not what you take it for –
now you've seen the animal inside,
the tooth ash, my legs thrash, the residue
of sounds from words I've never spoken, but should have.

*Note: Italicised phrases in 'Seizures' and 'Giving up Ground' were borrowed from *Lying* by Lauren Slater (2000).

Epilim Blues

– Epilim is an anticonvulsant medication used for the treatment of epilepsy in adults and children.

I found its meaning in Ancient Greek:
to seize, possess, afflict. And it was true,
it came down like the end of a knife.
When I had forgotten everything,
the doctor tripled my dose
so I couldn't feel the quivering
chords in my wrist. Slowly, Mum and I turned
and walked to the car, the script sweating
in my milky hand. I tried not to catch
her eyes. She was waiting for me.
We didn't say a word.
Just saw me standing there,
clutched me to her breast, as if to say:
we have a reason to cry.
The medley of medications taught
me to use everything I knew about jazz,
how to improvise. Only, I'd grown
too worn for comparisons;
fog was just fog.

'DEATH AND THE DOCTOR'

LEAH KAMINSKY

To dissect a cadaver is more than a simple mechanical exercise. It is a relationship – a dance in which the young student learns not only the hip-hop of anatomy, but also the tango of life and death. That first vision of the rigid reality of mortality stays branded in memory, a chilling reminder of what lies ahead, after all our 'hurry(ing) to get somewhere'. And as young doctors, the constant exposure to the dystopian world of illness and dying can render the body as 'something not quite human'.[40]

Poetry has a surgical eye. It can carve out meaning from despair and understanding from stupor. William Carlos Williams, a physician and poet, brought into relief the small beauty that can emerge from dis-ease – of thoughts of spring embedded in a simple red wheelbarrow – if the observer allows himself to notice important detail.[41] It is poetry that brings language to pain and suffering, giving voice to the silence or howled vowels of the sick. The poet works at the coalface of the living and the dying, a translator of the maladies of sinew and bone. And, most importantly, she holds empathy in her hands, refusing to allow it to evaporate into mere molecules. If only alongside the Hippocratic oath medical students were taught to recite the wisdom of the poets.

40 E. Kasket, 'Death and the Doctor – Existential Analysis', *Journal for the Society of Existential Analysis*, 17.1, January 2006.

41 W. C. Williams, 'The Red Wheelbarrow', in C. MacGowan, *The Collected Poems of William Carlos Williams, Volume I, 1909–1939*, New Directions Publishing, 1962.

The Wind Keeps Forgetting

the wind, in its hurry to get somewhere

doesn't see the spiderling wake at dawn
   carefully climb in concentric silk
around the spokes of its webs
   weaving crisscross to and fro
fastening itself in the middle
    to wait

the wind, in its hurry to get somewhere

collects twigs, dry leaves
   Snickers wrappers, torn Target catalogues
wears them like fancy dress
   over its invisible, shifting form
as if to laugh at a world so busy
   trying to hold on to its centre

Disorders of the Blood

His body trickles out of itself
as she stands slightly stooped
watching his blood congeal
this moment of separation
a huge, irredeemable mistake
yet, from today, she will have peace

Years since she bled
she remembers a time
his body was home
sweat and bare flesh
he holds her hand
between icy palms

Now, together again
in daylight dreams and mist
she watches him
his mind still hungry for life
eyes begging her to speak
of something he can't recall

their first kiss
a chorus of jackals in the valley
the neighbour singing arias in the shower
bulbuls screeching in the pine
the blue-crimson thread of veins
woven across her thighs

In Memoriam

What is a body, if not grace?
time worn, a book that can be read
a road map left so quietly by the dead
Legs that bore the weight of years
memory carved like etchings into skin
silken strands of wisdom line the heart

What is a man but specimen?
his name cleaved from the shell
that carried him through life
flesh, a rental car that drove him home

The not alive watch us through their lens
of time, waiting for the moment
when we gather them to us
to stand around them face to face and weep

we gaze upon the bodies of the dead
like children wading on the shores of lakes
not knowing just how deep they plunge
we dive like birds to open up the wound
and glimpse beyond the privacy of death
into the very wellspring of our lives

Let us speak then to the dead
thank them for their whitened bones
that galloped over fields of hay
and waltzed across the room by night

now dust has settled on the lids
of eyes that saw soft summer's light of day
and ears that heard the creaking of a door
strong hands that cradled infants, planted trees

beyond the firm umbrella of their flesh
follow quiet raindrops back in time

above and skyward bound
each drop returns to cloud
each cloud dissolving slowly into air
and air to space, with everything beyond

The dead enter our lives and trace
their memory stamped on teacups, rings and bears
paintings, vases, tables, chairs
we close their book
tears bathed in sacred space
What is a body, if not grace?

CONTRIBUTORS

Stuart Barnes was born in Hobart, Tasmania, and educated at Monash University, Victoria. His debut collection, *Glasshouses* (UQP, 2016), won the 2015 Arts Queensland Thomas Shapcott Poetry Prize. Stuart lives in Central Queensland and is poetry editor for *Tincture Journal*. His website is stuartabarnes.wordpress.com; he tweets @StuartABarnes.

Peter Boyle lives in Sydney. He is the author of seven collections of poetry, most recently *Ghostspeaking* (2016), *Towns in the Great Desert* (2013), and *Apocrypha* (2009) which won the Queensland Premier's Award in 2010. Among his other awards are the NSW Premier's Award (1995) and the South Australian Premier's Award (1998). As a translator of French and Spanish poetry he has had four books published, including *The Trees* (2005) by Venezuelan Eugenio Montejo and *Anima* (2011) by Cuban poet José Kozer. In 2013 he received the NSW Premier's Award for translation. He has presented his poetry at festivals in France, Quebec, El Salvador, Nicaragua, Colombia, Venezuela and Macedonia. His poetry has been translated into French, Spanish, Chinese and Swedish. He is currently completing a Doctorate of Creative Arts at the University of Western Sydney.

India Breen completed a Bachelor of Fine Arts in Creative and Professional Writing at the Queensland University of Technology in 2014. She is currently undertaking a Master of Fine Arts (Research) in Poetics at the Queensland University of Technology. She is the current poetry intern at *Island Magazine*. Her poetry and writing have appeared in *Southerly, Cordite, The Lifted Brow, Westerly, Stilts* and *Yen Magazine*. Her writing is an attempt at being wilfully honest, punchy and funny while showing evidence that deeper psychological/social considerations are in the subject of her work.

David Brooks is the co-editor of *Southerly* and Honorary Associate Professor at the University of Sydney. He was the 2015–16 Australia Council Fellow in fiction. His recent publications include *Napoleon's Roads* (stories; UQP

2016), *Open House* (poetry; UQP 2015) and *Derrida's Breakfast* (essays on poetry, philosophy and the animal; Brandl & Schlesinger 2016).

Anne M Carson is a writer and visual artist, who is published internationally and widely in Australia. *Removing the Kimono* was published by Hybrid Publishers in 2013. She has won and been commended in numerous poetry prizes including the 2015 Melbourne Poets Union International Poetry Prize. As a creative writing therapist, she has edited and facilitated the group process which resulted in the publication of three books. She serves as Director, Arts, on the board of Ondru – a social-change-through-the-creative-arts organisation. Currently she is looking for a publisher for the story in verse of a little-known Second World War humanitarian. The manuscript is called 'Massaging Himmler: a poetic biography of Dr Felix Kersten'. (www.annemcarson.com)

Grant Cochrane is an author and poet based in South East Queensland. His work has appeared or is forthcoming in various literary journals and anthologies, including *Southerly, Seizure, Snorkel, fourW* and *Bluepepper*. He is currently working on a collection of short stories.

Jessica Cohen is a freelance copyeditor, writer and social researcher, living in Melbourne. A trained psychotherapist, she is a keen observer of popular culture and the human condition, and a lover of art in many forms. She blogs at www.steppinginthegrey.com, where she writes about the private moments of beauty, anxiety and bewilderment which we all encounter; the undefinable, the transient and the uncomfortable things that give our lives meaning and sparkle. Jessica is currently developing a feminist magazine for pre-teen girls.

Meg Dunley is a writer and editor from Melbourne. She works at a secondary school in communications and marketing. She is currently completing her first young adult novel set in the near future where water is a precious commodity, and has another manuscript in the wings. She's been published in a number of anthologies, has been a journalist for her local paper for thirteen years and has blogged for over eight years about reading and writing, travelling in Australia with only a dinky old tent trailer and three boys, sustainability, sewing and life in general. She recently completed an Associate Degree of Professional Writing and Editing at RMIT, while wrangling her three teenage boys.

Dr Quinn Eades is a researcher, writer and poet whose work lies at the nexus of feminist, queer and trans theories of the body, autobiography and philosophy. His first book, *all the beginnings: a queer autobiography of the body*, was published by Tantanoola in 2015. He is a lecturer in Interdisciplinary Studies at La Trobe University, as well as the founding editor of Australia's only interdisciplinary, peer-reviewed, gender, sexuality and diversity studies journal, *Writing from Below*. He took home second prize in the prestigious and long-running Newcastle Poetry Prize for his poem 'Always going home (a domestic cycle)' in 2013, and another poem, 'Colder', was projected onto the side of a building in Krakow, Poland, for the 2014 International Lights Festival. He is currently working on an autobiography of his transitioning body titled 'Transpositions', and his first book of poetry, *Rallying*, is available now through UWA Publishing.

Steve Evans taught creative writing and literature at Flinders University until mid-2016 and now writes full-time. He is a reviewer, a literary editor for an international journal, has been on organising committees for seven literary festivals and a writer-in-residence in Australia, Singapore, New Zealand and Japan. Steve has been on arts funding and literary prize panels, and has won various poetry prizes, including the Queensland Premier's Poetry Prize. He has been a Barbara Hanrahan Fellow. He has written twelve books, including seven of poetry, and is currently working on further poetry collections and novels. He was raised mostly in South Australian country towns, which he counts as a real blessing. He is an avid motorcyclist and traveller.

Sophie Finlay is a librarian, visual artist and poet from Melbourne. She works as a branch librarian in a public library service. She has been a finalist in the John Leslie Art Prize and the Mt Buller Art Prize, and winner of the 'She Who Inspires' Art Prize at the Walker Street Gallery. She has exhibited in solo and group shows at the Fitzroy Gallery, the Frankston Arts Centre and the Brunswick Street Gallery. She studied visual and fine arts at the University of Melbourne. Her poetry has received highly commended and commended certificates in the W B Yeats Poetry Prize. She is currently juggling work, being a mum and studying an MA in Writing and Literature at Deakin University.

Ian Gibbins is a widely published poet, having recently retired after thirty-five years as a neuroscientist, twenty of which as Professor of Anatomy at Flinders University. His poetry explores a wide range of forms, often accompanied by his own electronic music and videos. (www.iangibbins. com.au)

Kevin Gillam is a West Australian writer with three books of poetry published: *Other Gravities* (2003) and *Permitted to Fall* (2007), both by Sunline Press, and *Songs Sul G* in *Two Poets* (Fremantle Press 2011). He works as Director of Music at Christ Church Grammar School in Perth.

Peter Goldsworthy has won literary awards across a wide range of genres, including the Commonwealth Poetry Prize, the 1988 Australian Bicentennial Poetry Prize, the FAW Christina Stead Award for fiction, and a Helpmann Award, with composer Richard Mills, for the opera *Batavia*. His 1995 novel *Wish* was recently rereleased in the Text Australian Classics series, and his 1989 novel *Maestro* as an Angus & Robertson Australian Classic. His most recent book, *The Rise of the Machines and Other Love Poems*, was published last year.

Rachael Guy is a multifaceted artist engaged in writing, performance and visual art. As well as writing, she creates puppet-based visual theatre for adults. She collaborated with poet Andy Jackson on 'Ambiguous Mirrors', a poetry/puppetry work which toured Ireland in 2013. Her creative writing has been published in journals and online, internationally and within Australia, and has featured in *Sleepers Almanac*, *Overland* and *Australian Poetry Journal*. In 2015 she was shortlisted for the Whitmore Press Manuscript Prize.

Susan Hawthorne is a poet, publisher, academic and translator. She is the author of eight collections of poetry, a verse novel, a novel and several nonfiction books. For many years she was an aerialist in two circuses and in recent years has turned her sights on extreme language learning (namely Sanskrit). Her collection *Cow* (2013) was shortlisted for the 2012 Kenneth Slessor Poetry Prize and a finalist for the 2012 Audre Lorde Lesbian Poetry Prize (USA), and *Earth's Breath* (2009) was shortlisted for the 2010 Judith Wright Poetry Prize. *Bird* and *Earth's Breath* were played on *Poetica* and her poetry has been translated into Chinese, Spanish, German and Indonesian. She has written extensively about her experience of epilepsy and the politics of disability. Her novel, *The Falling Woman* (1992), and collection of poems, *Bird and Other Writings on Epilepsy* (1999), focus on the theme of epilepsy, while her latest novel *Dark Matters* (2017) is a meditation on pain. Her nonfiction includes, among others, an article in the anthology *Radically Speaking* (1996) and an essay in US magazine *Trivia*. For more information, visit www.spinifexpress.com.au and susanslambdawolfblog. blogspot.com.au.

Andy Jackson was shortlisted for the 2011 Kenneth Slessor Prize for his poetry collection *Among the Regulars* (Papertiger). He won the 2013 Whitmore Press Manuscript Prize with *The Thin Bridge*. His most recent book, *Immune Systems* (Transit Lounge), explores medical tourism in India. A forthcoming collection, *Music Our Bodies Can't Hold*, consists of portraits of other people with Marfan syndrome. 'Ambiguous Mirrors', a puppetry/ poetry collaboration with Rachael Guy, toured Ireland in 2013. He blogs irregularly at amongtheregulars.wordpress.com.

gareth roi jones is a member of the Dandylion Collective, a small writers' group based in Adelaide. He has published a solo collection *Gunyah Healing* (Wakefield Press 2012), and in 2014 he co-edited *The Infinite Dirt* (FSP 38). He has been slowly garnering success in numerous competitions: 'glamoured' was highly commended and 'interstellar heron' was shortlisted in the Interstellar Award for Speculative Poetry; 'full moon feast' and 'slumber' were both commended for the 2014 W B Yeats Poetry Prize for Australia; and more. He has also been published in various journals and anthologies. He was a spoken word SA 2016 poet-in-residence at the Adelaide City Council, City Library.

Leah Kaminsky is a physician and award-winning writer. She is the Poetry and Fiction Editor at the *MJA* and a contributing writer at *Panorama – the Journal of Intelligent Travel*. Her debut novel, *The Waiting Room*, won the Voss Literary Prize in 2016 (Vintage Australia 2015; Harper Perennial US 2016). Her poetry collection, *Stitching Things Together,* was shortlisted for the Anne Elder Award. Her poem, *In Memoriam*, was a finalist for the Hippocrates Poetry Prize. *We're all Going to Die* has been described as 'a joyful book about death' (Harper Collins 2016). She edited *Writer MD* (Knopf US, starred on Booklist) and co-authored *Cracking the Code* (Vintage 2015). She holds an MFA from Vermont College of Fine Arts. (leahkaminsky.com)

Kristen Lang writes in North West Tasmania. Her first collection, *Let Me Show You a Ripple*, combines poems and photographs and reflects an ongoing interest – how each medium can place us inside a small, expanding moment. A framed fragment can take us further than its own devices seem rightly to allow. There are words for what isn't in the words. Images that let us see the world a little differently. This is what draws her to poetry. She continues to write, and has two collections forthcoming in 2017. She lives in the foothills of Mount Roland with her husband and their dog.

Sid Larwill has never before described himself as a writer, although he definitely writes. He has authored or co-authored five scientific papers, and written over one hundred unpublished scientific reports. He has an unpublished novel in his bottom drawer, but suspects it might be better as a haiku. Poetry is a form he loves, but writes only rarely. He once described himself as the world's leading expert on the behavioural ecology of Sloane's froglet, an inconspicuous little frog that chirps away in Northern Victorian swamps and wetlands. He hasn't heard one for a long time. And that makes him a little sad. He lives in Castlemaine. And that makes him a little happy.

Rachael Mead is a South Australian poet. She has an Honours degree in Classical Archaeology, a Master's in Environmental Studies and a PhD in Creative Writing from the University of Adelaide. She is the author of three collections of poetry: *Sliding Down the Belly of the World* (Wakefield Press 2012), *The Sixth Creek* (Picaro Press 2013) and *The Quiet Blue World* (Garron Publishing 2015). You can find more of her work at rachaelmead.com.

Gretta Jade Mitchell recently completed a creative writing research degree which won the Dean's Commendation for Master's Thesis Excellence, and is starting work on her first novel. She has been published in *TEXT*, *Writing from Below*, *SOd press*, and *Gargouille*.

Rachel Robertson is a senior lecturer at Curtin University in Western Australia. She is the author of the memoir *Reaching One Thousand* and co-editor of *Purple Prose*, a collection of essays by women writers. Her research interests include Australian literature, critical disability studies and writing about illness, disability and loss. She can be contacted at R.Robertson@curtin.edu.au.

Margaret Owen Ruckert is an educator and poet, and won the 2012 IP Poetry Book of the Year for *musefood*. She is widely published and a previous winner of the NSW Women Writers National Poetry Award. She is the facilitator of Discovery Writers, and gives monthly writing workshops, still inspired by her mature-age Master's degree. Her first book *You Deserve Dessert* explored sweet foods through poetry.

Ian C. Smith lives in Sale, Victoria, the last of thirty-two places he has lived, has travelled to twenty-five countries, and worked at forty jobs, from football coach to photographer, trainee textile mechanic to teacher. Additionally, 711 of his poems, short stories, essays and reviews have been published in 179 different Australian titles, and in 162 different titles in nineteen other countries, journals, newspapers, radio, etc., and even translated into Japanese. He has won fifty first prizes in literary competitions, mainly for poetry and short stories, and received three grants from Arts Victoria and the Literature Board of Australia. He has written seven books, all published by Ginninderra Press, the most recent: *Wonder Sadness Madness Joy* (2014). Despite all this, he feels he has wasted too much of life and would love another crack at it. He compiles records, counts everything, an obsession like writing, and is afraid of forgetting.

Beth Spencer writes poetry, fiction and essays. Her most recent books are *Vagabondage* (UWAP 2014), a verse memoir about a year she spent living in a campervan, and *The Party of Life*, a bilingual (English–Chinese) collection from Flying Islands / ASM in 2015. Previous awards include *The Age* Short Story Award, the inaugural Dinny O'Hearn Fellowship, and runner-up for the Steele Rudd Award for *How to Conceive of a Girl* (fiction, Random House 1996). After a long gap between books, she is pleased to be publishing again. She also has a PhD and is a creativity coach using EFT (Emotional Freedom Technique). She lives on the Central Coast of NSW and has a website at www.bethspencer.com.

Heather Taylor Johnson published her fourth book of poetry, *Meanwhile, the Oak*, with Five Islands Press. Her second novel is *Jean Harley was Here*, out with UQP. She is the poetry editor for *Transnational Literature* and has been reviewing poetry (also prose and other art forms, especially film) for more than fifteen years. She has a PhD in Creative Writing from the

University of Adelaide. She is hugely indebted to the Richard Llewellyn Deaf and Disability Arts fund.

Rob Walker has long been fascinated by language. In between his time as an educator in performing arts around Adelaide, South Australia, and teaching English to junior and senior high students and adults in Japan, he has also found time to write a children's musical, essays, short stories, poetry reviews, co-edit a poetry anthology and produce four poetry collections and two chapbooks. With hundreds of poems published online and in journals and anthologies in the UK, US and Australia (including *Best Australian Poems*), he also enjoys collaborating with other artists (Max-Mo, Zephyr Quartet and ccmixter.org). His audio-essay 'Civility in Japan' was broadcast on ABC Radio National's *Ockham's Razor*. He currently divides his time between grandchildren, a small farm in the Adelaide Hills, travelling, writing, enjoying his orchard, making his own wine, playing the shakuhachi and listening to jazz.

Fiona Wright is a writer, editor and critic from Sydney. Her book of essays *Small Acts of Disappearance* won the 2016 Queensland Literary Award for nonfiction and the Kibble Award, and was shortlisted for the Stella Prize and the NSW Premier's Douglas Stewart Award for nonfiction . Her poetry collection, *Knuckled*, won the 2012 Dame Mary Gilmore Award. She has recently completed a PhD at Western Sydney University's Writing and Society Research Centre.

ACKNOWLEDGEMENTS

Stuart Barnes

'Cups' was published in *Glasshouses* (2016, UQP, St Lucia) and *The Canberra Times* (2016, Fairfax Media, Canberra).

'Endone' was published in *Glasshouses* (2016, UQP, St Lucia).

Peter Boyle

'Paralysis' was published in *What the Painter Saw in Our Faces*, Wollongong: Five Islands Press, 2001.

'On the eternal nature of fresh beginnings' was published in *Southerly* 76.2, 2017.

'On the eternal nature of fresh beginnings' and 'Hammerblows' were published in *Ghostspeaking*, Sydney: Vagabond Press, 2016.

India Breen

'Epilim Blues,' and 'Giving up Ground' were published in *Southerly* 76.2, 2017.

David Brooks

'Spiders About the House' appeared in *Meanjin* 70.1 (2012) and was first published in book form in *Open House* (UQP 2015).

Quinn Eades

'Coalesce', 'Absorption', and 'Reverberation' were published in *Rallying*, UWA Publishing, WA, 2017.

'Coalesce' was published in *Cordite: the End* (53.0) 2016. (cordite.org.au/poetry/theend/coalesce/).

'Reverberation' was published in *Southerly* 76.2, 2017.

Ian Gibbins

'cataplexy' in *e•ratio 21* (2015); ed., Gregory Vincent St Thomasino; New York. (www.eratiopostmodernpoetry.com/issue21_Gibbins.html.)

'Sometimes It Hurts' in *Flying Kites: Friendly Street Poets 36*, p. 52; eds, Judy Dally & Louise McKenna, Adelaide (2012).

Kevin Gillam
'propped' was published in *Southerly*, 74.2, 2014, University of Sydney Press.

Rachael Guy
A version of 'Discontinuation' appeared in *Negative Capability*, Volume 34: The Body in D[ist]ress, 2016.

Susan Hawthorne
'Eurydice' is published in *Bird and Other Writings on Epilepsy*, Spinifex Press, North Melbourne, 1999, p. 46.
'descent' is published in *Lupa and Lamb*, Spinifex Press, North Melbourne, 2014, p. 3.

Andy Jackson
'Nothing personal' is published in *Among the regulars*, Andy Jackson, West End, Qld: Papertiger Media, 2010.
'Whatever exists in the universe' is published in *Immune Systems*, Andy Jackson, Melbourne: Transit Lounge, 2015.
'Jess' is published in *Music Our Bodies Can't Hold*, St Lucia, Qld: Hunter Publishers, 2017.

Leah Kaminsky
'In Memoriam' was a finalist in the 2016 Hippocrates Poetry Prize. It was shortlisted for the Canberra Health Poetry Prize.

Ian C. Smith
'The poet as ageing narcissist' was published in *Wonder Sadness Madness Joy*, Ginninderra Press, Port Adelaide, 2014.
'Post-coital repercussion' was published in *Memory Like Hunger*, Ginninderra Press, Charnwood, ACT, 2006.
'Surgery' was published in *Rabbit Journal*, no. 18, 2016.

Beth Spencer
'The Shipwreck Coast' and 'To the Whales at Warrnambool' were first published in *Vagabondage* (Perth: UWAP, 2014).

Heather Taylor Johnson

'The Sick Room' was published in *The Medical Journal of Australia*, 2015; 203(2): 118. (www.mja.com.au/system/files/issues/203_02/tay00443.pdf.)

'Trying to Write about Ménière's Disease' was published in *Southerly* 76.2, 2017. It was shortlisted for the Canberra Health Poetry Prize.

Rob Walker

'radiology' was first published in *Policies & Procedures*, Southern-Land Poets, Garron Publishing. A later version (a collaboration with Magdalena Ball) appeared in *Medical Journal of Australia*, vol. 204, issue 7 (18 April 2016) (www.mja.com.au/journal/2016/204/7/radiology) and in *Best Australian Science Writing 2016,* UNSW Press (November 2016).

'extra-corporeal shockwave therapy' was first published in *Policies & Procedures*, Southern-Land Poets, Garron Publishing (2016).

Lightning Source UK Ltd.
Milton Keynes UK
UKHW040743140819
347957UK00003B/761/P